MW01181135

INSIDE OUT

*a catalyst
for conscious living*

Dan Coughlin

POS Publishing
St. Louis, MO

Published by POS Publishing
ISBN   0-9648770-0-7

This book is dedicated to those people whose goal is to actually live the life they consciously want to live.

Table of Contents

INITIATIVE

EPILOGUE

Acknowledgments

My mom (Laura) and dad (Gene); my brother, Kevin, his wife, Sue, and their daughter Kaylee; my sister, Cathy; my brother, Jim, his wife, Liz, and their daughters, Juliana, Mariel, and Leah; my brother, Mick; and my sister, MaryEileen. You have each taught me so much about really loving and caring for other people. You have inspired me through your words and examples.

My special teachers and coaches: Nancy Wondrach, Tom Becvar, Ebbie Dunn, Dennis Grace, and Andrea Rothbart. You believed in me even when I didn't.

My professional mentors: Ted Drewes, Stanley "Butch" Perchan, Jean Ponsetto, Jerry Yeagley, and Tom Becvar. Through your example, you taught me priceless lessons on how to deal with people and run an organization.

My bookcover designer, Christina Ensign. Thank you for the patience and creativity you poured into the cover of this book. My editor, MaryAnne Brooks. Thank you for being so thorough in guiding this book to the finish line. My advisor in the publishing process, Shep Hyken, and my first teacher in the world of professional speaking, Tom Pall. Thank you for your support and your ideas.

My special friends who have supported this project: E. Laine, Carib Martin, Shirley Martin, Mike and Joyce Feder, Pat Carr, Craig Hannick, and Barb Bizer. Your support made this book possible and I am very grateful.

My best friend, Jeff Hutchison, who supported all of my dreams for the last fifteen years and read all five editions that this book went through before it was published. Thanks for all of your advice. I wish everyone could have a best friend like you.

Introduction

We sometimes live like we are trying to pick up a small object in a very dark room. We measure our success as a human being by our salary, material possessions, and our children's achievements. We determine our self-worth by our current position on some arbitrary, societal scale. We reach for praise and labels to provide us with lasting happiness. Rather than approaching life from the external perspective of other people's opinions, why don't we turn the light switch on and consciously make decisions based on our own internal standards?

I struggled with the external perspective for many years. I worked very hard to impress others and always felt empty at the end of my efforts. As a result, I searched for and discovered an approach to living that helps us experience the personal life, relationships, and career we consciously want. I call this "Inside-Out Living". The purpose of this book is to help you live the life you consciously want to live.

Before we go any further, I want to clarify some of my basic conclusions. I do not have the answers for anyone else on how to achieve success and happiness. I don't know of any method for motivating someone to do something they don't want to do. I am not playing the role of your teacher. I don't have the answers for you, but I believe you do. I believe each of us has our own unique set of success principles and the ability to put them into action. I do not see myself as your personal success coach. If anything, I see myself more as your assistant coach. Assistant coaches make suggestions while head coaches make decisions. You are your own head coach. You make the final decisions in your life. I do see myself performing the role of a catalyst. If you mix the thoughts in this book with your own ideas, you will speed up the process of identifying and achieving your desires.

The first part of this book focuses on personal integrity. We live with integrity when our thoughts, words, and actions

Introduction

match our consciously selected values, beliefs, desires, and principles. Even though we will endure some very painful moments, we move toward the life we consciously want by living with integrity. People who always follow their subconscious programming allow other people to choose their standards. They refuse to reflect on what they think, say, and do. These people never identify the life they really want to experience.

The second part of this book concentrates on personal initiative. When we act with personal initiative, we consciously select our objectives. We choose the direction of our life rather than allowing others to do so for us. Even though competitive people go to extraordinary lengths to achieve more than someone else, they feel disillusioned when they see themselves chasing after someone else's dream. People with initiative avoid this internal conflict by moving toward their own goals.

Personal integrity and initiative emphasize the uniqueness of every individual. I believe you have the ability within you to create the personal life, relationships, and career you consciously want to experience.

INTEGRITY

The Fundamentals of Inside-Out Thinking

The next eight chapters contain many of the key concepts and definitions in this philosophy of inside-out thinking. I encourage you to maintain an on-going debate with these ideas by writing in the margins what you agree with, disagree with, think would be a more helpful idea, and why you feel this way. The more actively you participate in this discussion, the more effectively you will use these ideas and create your own success principles.

Outside-In

Outside-in people follow the opinions of other people without any regard to their own ideas.

Personal Characteristics

Outside-in people turn the control of their lives over to other people. They follow orders at all times. They ignore any internal conflicts with the plans given them. When more than one person directs them at the same time, they follow the loudest or the most powerful person. They avoid responsibility. If anything goes wrong, they quickly point out that they did what others told them to do.

Outside-in individuals make decisions based solely on their subconscious programming. They choose to eat healthy or fattening food, but they base these choices on childhood habits or the latest trend in society. They refuse to identify or pursue their own goals.

Outside-in thinkers desperately want to impress other people. They go along with every idea in the hope of gaining approval. Because they don't accept themselves as they are, they do and say whatever it takes for others to accept them. They develop their minds, bodies, and personalities to draw attention from other people. Their feelings of self-worth only come from other people's positive feedback. They maintain low self-esteem because they see themselves as having no inherent worth.

Outside-in people have no constancy of purpose. They change their points of view whenever they run into new opinions. Not only do they follow others, they frequently change their leaders. They fail to achieve lasting importance because they never stick with one definite purpose. Since they never choose their own paths, their lives don't stand for anything.

Outside-in people use up their time and energy worrying about the criticisms and judgments of other people. They hate being seen in a negative way by another person. They continually compare their achievements with other people in the hope of being "better" at something than someone else. They gossip about and tear other people down. They focus on short-term approval in the form of salaries, promotions, and compliments.

Outside-in people define a "significant life" as impressing a large number of people. They measure their significance by their level of fame and popularity.

Organizational Characteristics

While outside-in thinking is a personal orientation, we see it demonstrated in our families, schools, and careers.

Family

Outside-in families hone the skills of comparing accomplishments, criticizing decisions, and competing against others. The individual members cut off their natural selves and allow other people to program them toward specific career, social, and relationship roles. Based on their status within the family, they carry false feelings of inferiority or superiority into one experience after another.

Outside-in parents reveal their true orientation at their children's events. They place greater value on their child's victory, playing time, and performance than on the child's development as a human being. One of the saddest stories I remember as a coach happened when a goalkeeper let in several goals in one soccer game, and his father wouldn't talk to him for a week. These parents measure their self-worth by their children's performances. They willingly attack the teacher, moderator, coach, or director when they feel their child did not receive the opportunity to impress other people. They convey the message that their children are important only because of what they do rather than because they are unique and special human beings.

Outside-in individuals look to marry someone with the proper labels. They marry another person to make themselves look better. They want the other person's money, career, or attractiveness, but they show little interest in their spouse's desires.

Education

Outside-in people primarily use education to build a resume for a particular high school, college, or career. They perform the ultimate act of trying to impress people they have never met.

Outside-in students base the value of their education on their grade point average, class rank, and starting salary. They join projects to increase their labels. They don't care whether they learn anything from the experience or not. They view education as the "grade game". They feel someone must win and someone must lose in every situation. Outside-in teachers, administrators, government officials, and parents perpetuate this mentality by preparing students to be efficient workers rather than confident and caring human beings.

Career

Outside-in thinkers want to impress other people with their careers. They set aside their integrity for promotions. They focus obsessively on externals: title, office size, and the number of people reporting to them. They take positions purely for greater salaries rather than standing for what they believe in. They need other people to tell them they are successful. They constantly change their career plans and vacillate from one objective to another. The organizations they lead set aside long-term development for the prospect of immediate rewards and quick profits.

Inside-Out

Inside-out people make decisions based on their consciously selected values, beliefs, desires, and principles.

Personal Characteristics

Inside-out people take control of their own lives. They listen to other people's opinions and adapt these ideas to their own situations when they feel it is appropriate. They always identify what they want and go after it.

Inside-out people accept full responsibility for their actions. Since they base their decisions on their own principles, they don't blame other people for the results. They realize they made their own choices and accept the consequences.

Inside-out thinkers concentrate on self-respect. They challenge new ideas by thinking about them for a long time. Only when they see the true merit in these ideas do they endorse them. They remain genuine and sincere in every scenario. They possess high levels of personal integrity.

Inside-out people want honest feedback from other people, but they use it only as indicators for how they might improve. They feel their own ideas and opinions matter as much as those of anyone else.

They maintain a high sense of self-esteem because their feelings of worth come from within them. They accept other people for who they are because they accept themselves.

Inside-out thinkers serve as leaders by carefully building a sense of purpose and staying true to it. They stick to a definite cause and achieve lasting importance. They communicate their purpose clearly and consistently. They realize they never control another person's decisions. They care deeply about other people and support them in making their own choices.

Inside-out people concentrate on continual growth. They search for ways to improve the quality of their decisions by

Inside-Out

refining their purpose and improving the process of reaching it. They develop their minds, bodies, and personalities to help them reach their purpose.

Inside-out people define a "significant life" as experiencing the personal life, relationships, and career they consciously want. They measure their degree of significance by how well they stand up for what they believe in.

Organizational Characteristics
Inside-out thinkers impact their families, schools, and careers.

Family
Inside-out families openly and honestly discuss their values, beliefs, desires, and principles. They encourage members to choose their own foundations. Individuals ask each other questions and listen empathetically to find the reasons behind the other person's decisions. Members select their unique paths in life. Everyone determines what they want, why they want it, and how they will achieve it.

Inside-out families emphasize consistent reflection on what they did, why they did it, and what they learned from the situation. They base their family experiences on communication. They sincerely express their feelings and the specific reasons underlying them.

Inside-out parents help their child use external activities as a medium for developing their mind, body, and personality. They guide their children to find the lesson within the experience. Regardless of the outcome, these children mature as they go through one activity after another.

Inside-out couples invest vulnerability, commitment, time, and energy into their relationship. They focus on communicating honestly, remaining aware of the reasons

Inside-Out

beneath their feelings, and expressing these feelings in a sincere manner. They see their relationship as a means for helping each other develop internally. As they learn to love, care for, and support the other person, they learn how to love, care for, and support themselves. They remain true to their own values and beliefs while respecting the other person's decisions.

Education

Inside-out students use group discussions and personal reflection time to select their personal values, beliefs, desires, and principles. They identify their personal assets, past successes, and specific objectives. They determine their own sense of right and wrong. They attempt to live with personal integrity. They develop self-confidence and self-discipline. They use academic courses, athletics, and active experiences in the fine arts to enhance their communication skills through reading, writing, listening, speaking, performing, and creating. They develop the ability to think logically and intuitively. They continually improve their physical health and personalities. They clarify a definite purpose for their current lives and communicate this purpose to other people. They attempt to live the lives they consciously want to live.

Inside-out teachers and administrators create an environment for personal development. They set aside time in the school day for students to reflect on their past achievements, personal strengths, and dreams for the future. They encourage students to question the values, beliefs, desires, and principles of our society and decide for themselves what they stand for. They use grades as feedback in helping students improve their process of learning and communicating what they have learned. They do not compare students to one another. They emphasize the uniqueness and dignity of every individual.

Inside-Out

Career

Inside-out thinkers use their careers as a means for expressing what they stand for. They select a definite purpose for their work and pour themselves into achieving this purpose. Their jobs may vary during their careers, but they remain true to their purpose. They maintain their personal integrity even if it costs them their current position. They trade short-term profits, promotions, and prestige for long-term effectiveness. The organizations they lead make lasting and significant contributions to society.

Many of us go back and forth between outside-in and inside-out thinking. This book contains ideas, definitions, and strategies for helping us live from the inside-out.

When did you approach situations from the outside-in and the inside-out? How did you feel after each experience?

Human Spirit

Our human spirit provides us with the means for consciously creating the life we want to live.

When someone overcomes enormous odds, we call it a triumph of the human spirit. This statement stirs up a number of questions. What makes up the human spirit? How does our human spirit create achievements? How do we consciously direct our human spirit toward specific objectives?

The Four Dimensions of the Human Spirit

Our human spirit has four parts: spirit, mind, personality, and body.

Spirit

Our spirit represents the internal energies governing our decisions. I often refer to our spirit as our "governing energies". These energies direct our mind, body, and personality. Several different aspects make up our spirit. Each contributes toward guiding our thoughts, words, and actions.

I call our values, beliefs, principles, and desires the essence of our spirit. I frequently use the word "essence" to replace these four words. Our values are what we perceive as being important. Our beliefs form our expectations for the future. Our principles are the rules we use for making decisions. Our desires serve as the basis for our goals.

Our emotions sometimes override our essence. They strengthen, diminish, and change our values. They generate us into action or stop us from moving. We shift our decisions because of anger, fear, worry, exhaustion, hatred, and depression. Worrying about our children and feeling stress in our relationships may cause us to realign our career desires. Our pride often keeps us from taking a position we really want.

Human Spirit

Our sexual energy is closely tied to our creative energy. The way we choose to express this energy makes a tremendous difference in our future accomplishments. Our sexual energy causes us to endanger our personal life, relationships, and career when we pour it into pornography, affairs, and prostitution. If we deliberately direct our sexual energy toward enhancing our relationships and creatively achieving meaningful objectives, we move toward inside-out significance.

Our intuition represents the messages we receive from our inner voice. I believe these impulses concerning our personal life, relationships, and career come to us through a divine higher power. When we trust our intuition, we follow through on these messages and take action.

Addictions to alcohol, drugs, food, sex, spending, and work obliterate our essence. Our addictions direct us toward decisions we would never consciously make. We may feel helpless in the face of these addictions and incapable of regaining control of our decisions.

In summary, our spirit includes the governing energies of our essence, emotions, sexual/creative energy, intuition, and addictions.

Mind

Our mind interprets the messages from our spirit and translates them into plans for our personality through two main methods.

In the first method, we logically determine how we will enact this message in a step-by-step process. We base our decisions on whether or not they logically fit in with the previous step. If we receive a message to value our family more, we write down this objective and why it is important to us. We determine where we have neglected our family and how we will improve in this area. We write a specific plan of when and where we will

14

spend more time with each member. We set specific goals for listening better and making eye contact more often. As the weeks go by, we refer to our plan, reflect on the short-term outcomes, and make the necessary adjustments.

In the second method, we operate on our instincts. We see the whole picture in our mind and instinctively take action. We don't wait for specific reasons or for a long-range plan. If we receive an impulse to value our family more, we instinctively pick up the phone and call our brother, set up a lunchdate with our parents, or volunteer to babysit our niece. We do what we feel is the right thing to do at that moment.

Personality

Our personality interprets and expresses the messages it receives from our mind. Several people receive the same message and express it in totally different ways. Our personality styles determine how we learn and express ideas. These styles vary greatly from one person to another and from one situation to another. Individual personality needs include achieving goals, feeling accepted, receiving attention, and analyzing information. If their particular needs are not met, the individual will find it difficult to learn or express new ideas. Some people focus on feelings over logic, intuition over facts, and long-term dreams over short-term decisions. Other people do just the opposite. Some individuals experience a surge of energy when they go inward while others gain this energy burst by interacting with people.

Body

Our body communicates the messages it receives from our personality through our facial expressions, body stance, tone of voice, physical movements, and words. Our personality may choose to listen empathetically, but the way in which our body

Human Spirit

expresses this decision determines the way our intention comes across. If we sit fifteen feet away from the other person and don't make eye contact, we send out one message. If we sit on the same couch with the other person and look straight into his or her eyes, we send out another message. Our body perfoms the final role of the human spirit by expressing our governing energies to other people.

The Human Spirit
Creates Achievements

All four dimensions play an important role within the system of the human spirit. Our spirit develops a specific energy. Once this energy becomes strong enough, it is subconsciously or consciously sent onto our mind. Our mind interprets this energy and translates it into a message for our personality. Our personality physically expresses this message through our body.

We see how the system of the human spirit operates through the following two analogies. At the performance of a symphony, the sheet music represents the spirit. It sends a specific message to the conductor. The conductor, representing the mind, interprets the music and translates it for the musicians. The musicians, representing the personality, express the translation from the conductor. The instruments, representing the body, implement the expression of the musicians. Each part is equally important in the overall performance. On a professional football team, the head coach represents the spirit. He sends a specific energy to the assistant coaches. He wants a particular gameplan and team attitude. The assistant coaches, representing the mind, interpret this gameplan and translate it for their particular players. The players, representing the personality, express what they have learned to the best of their ability. They use their bodies and equipment, representing the body, to implement this expression.

Human Spirit

We see how the system of the human spirit creates achievements through the following example. We watch a film that reminds us of how much we value our friends. Our spirit highlights this value. This governing energy flows through our mind where it mentally interprets this message as,"I need to show my friends how much I care about them" and translates it into an action plan as,"I will write these people several honest and sincere letters." Our personality decides how to express our feelings in the form of words. Our body carries this impulse through the physical act of writing the words on paper. Our human spirit has given birth to another achievement: several written letters to our close friends.

Consciously Guiding Our Human Spirit

Every achievement comes about as the result of a specific governing energy flowing through our human spirit. We guide our human spirit toward achieving specific objectives by consciously choosing the governing energy we send onto our mind. When we consciously determine our essence, emotions, and the way we use our sexual/creative energy, trust our intuition, and direct our addictions, we choose what our life stands for and what we will achieve both internally and externally. If we want greater peace of mind, we start by believing we are capable of greater internal balance. If we want a more enjoyable family life, we highlight how much we value our parents, siblings, and children. If we want a happier marriage, we set listening to our spouse as a specific desire. If we want our career to stand for something specific, we choose the career principles that we will base our decisions on.

The next two chapters contain more ideas on consciously guiding our governing energy.

Conscious Choices

We make conscious choices by deliberately selecting our governing energies.

Making Conscious Decisions

We make conscious choices in three steps. First, we identify the governing energies we currently use. Second, we decide which ones we agree with and want to keep and which ones we disagree with and want to change. Third, we consciously select the energies we want guiding our decisions.

By writing down what we value in our personal life, relationships, and career, we identify why we did something or why we want to do it. After we go through these values one at a time, we decide to keep them the same or change them. As we change our underlying values, we prepare the way for new decisions. We may value eating fried food for social reasons, as a reward for working hard, to deal with anxiety or guilt, or as something to do while we watch TV. We may consume fattening food because it provides us with immediate satisfaction or because we ate this type of food as a child. After we examine all of the reasons why we eat certain types of food, we consciously select the values we want to base our eating on. If we decide to value food as fuel for our body, we automatically base our eating habits on improving the amount of energy we have throughout the day. When we use this method, we consciously choose what we eat. We deliberately guide our essence by following this same process for our beliefs, principles, and desires.

We identify our governing emotions by mentally going into one of our daily situations and observing our feelings. After we see our emotional patterns, we decide to keep using these emotions or change to new ones. Since our emotions guide us, we make conscious choices by deliberately selecting the ones we want generating our decisions. When we mentally place ourself with certain people, we feel angry or frustrated. These

Conscious Choices

emotions guide us toward acting rude and sarcastic. If we consciously choose to feel comfortable and caring, we will listen closely and try to understand the other person's point of view. We shift our actions by changing the underlying emotions.

Creating Our Conscious Cushions

When we overwhelm ourself with activities, we base our decisions on our past programming and the opinions of other people. We do this without any conscious input of our own in the decision-making process. We regain control of our decisions by creating a cushion of mental space that separates our subconscious programming from our decisions. Within this space, we consciously choose what we will do and why we will do it.

We visualize our conscious cushion by imagining ourself sitting in the middle of a square room on a chair that is ten feet from each of the walls. Pictures hang all over the walls. These pictures represent all the possible decisions we can choose at any given moment. As we sit in the chair, we receive subconscious impulses to make a certain decision. We want to make this decision immediately, but we have to walk ten feet to the wall and select the picture which matches this impulse. The space between the chair and the wall represents our conscious cushion. Within these ten feet, we deliberately choose our values, beliefs, principles, desires, and emotions and alter our future decisions. By visualizing ourself within this mental cushion, we break the connection between our subconscious programming and our decisions. We use this mental space to take control of our governing energies and make new decisions.

We maintain our conscious cushions by getting a sufficient amount of rest, eating properly, excercising regularly, spending time in nature, reading and listening to inspiring ideas and music, and quietly reflecting on the events of the day.

Conscious Choices

We only make conscious choices for improvement when we know what we want improved. If we keep track of our spending patterns for one year, we see where our money goes. As a result, we make adjustments and take control of our finances. When we increase our awareness of the problems in our personal life, relationships, and career and why they happen, we widen our conscious cushions and find ways for solving them.

What decisions do you make based on your subconscious programming that you will consciously alter?

Personal Powers

Our personal powers represent the tools we have within us for consciously guiding our governing energies.

Powers lie inherent within each of us. By using them, we create our own destiny. When we neglect them, we forfeit the life we consciously want to live.

Some Personal Powers

We choose to live consciously or we allow our subconscious programming to control us. We deliberately choose our essence, emotions, and the way we use our sexual energy or we allow other people to choose them for us. The choice is ours.

When we study our past to understand why we took certain actions, we increase our power in the present. By recalling our success stories, we gain confidence for taking on new challenges. When we recall our unsuccessful attempts, we turn mistakes into useful lessons.

We commit ourself to action by announcing our objectives. When we proclaim our goals and stamp our name on a project, we direct our efforts toward achieving these goals.

We achieve an enormous variety of meaningful objectives during our lifetime, but we can't do everything. By prioritizing our values and desires, we automatically guide our efforts toward fulfilling them. We live a significant life by working on the goals which coincide with our highest priorities.

Patience allows us to stick to our plan even when we don't immediately reach the external results we want. Patience allows us to achieve long-term goals that we could not accomplish without it.

Our perspective determines our emotions. We instantly change our emotions by altering our perspective. We feel angry toward our parents if we see them as trying to control us. If we change our perspective and see our parents as doing their best to help us improve, we feel cared for and loved.

We surround a situation in awareness by using the twin powers of previewing and reviewing. By previewing a situation, we locate exactly what we want to accomplish and why we want to do it. We choose the specific values, beliefs, principles, desires, and emotions we will use and the way we will use them. We see the obstacles standing in our way and visualize what it will take to deal with them. After the situation has been created, we review our efforts by asking specific questions. Did we stick to the governing energies we had selected? What governing energies do we keep the same and which ones do we change? Did we express our ideas in the way we wanted to express them? Do we still want to fulfill our original purpose? If not, what do we change to? How do we create this change?

We guide our emotions by saying specific phrases. If we need to stop procrastinating, we say,"Do it now" and jump into action. By using this famous self-starter, we focus on the value of immediately moving toward our objective. We guide our spirit by saying,"This too shall pass", "One day at a time", "Easy does it", "Carpe diem, seize the day", "First things first", and "Just do it".

We consciously wake ourself up from our subconscious slumber by interrupting our patterns. I used to pour butter all over a piece of toast before I ate it. I valued eating properly and staying in good shape, but I would heap huge amounts of butter on rolls, danishes, and bread. I realized my actions contradicted my values, but I would still do it without thinking about it. I needed a patternbreaker to interrupt my subconscious thoughts and force me to think consciously. I started saying, "Butter, butter, butter, butter, butter, butter, butter!" every time I picked up my knife for butter. This patternbreaker forced me to make a conscious decision. Did I want to keep pouring butter into my

Personal Powers

system or did I want to stop? After using this patternbreaker many times, I consciously developed a new habit. I haven't used butter on my toast in over five years.

We raise our awareness by asking point-blank questions. Do our thoughts, words, and actions reflect the essence and emotions that we really want to base our decisions on? Does our personal life, relationships, and career match what we consciously desire? How will we improve them? Are we expressing our thoughts in ways that we feel are appropriate?

What personal powers will you use to take control of your decisions?

Magnets

Magnets represent the subconscious voices pulling us toward certain thoughts, words, and actions.

In the same way a magnet pulls some objects toward it and repels others, our subconscious programming pulls us toward specific outcomes and away from others. Our magnets come from a variety of sources. We first encounter these magnets during childhood and continue to face them through adolescence and adulthood.

Our families, peers, and supervisors serve as magnetic resources. They communicate their values through their praise, criticism, and evaluations. They impact our subconscious through their actions, attitudes, relationships, and views on money, sex, alcohol, marriage, and careers. Our subconscious soaks all of this information in and sends it onward to our spirit. Without our realizing it, these subconscious voices attempt to guide our decisions every single day.

People we have never met form another type of magnet. Television shows, magazines, radio programs, and newspapers constantly barrage us with value-laden statements about what "society" considers fashionable and newsworthy. Films, music, sports, and theatrical performances portray certain values, principles, beliefs, and points of view. We subconsciously store this information like a dam trapping the energy of a river.

Magnets devastate our ability to reach our objectives by pulling us toward particular governing energies. They tell us what type of person we should marry, the career we should have, the amount of money we need, how much we should weigh, the clothes we should wear, and what we should look like. We cannot lead the life we consciously desire until we remove the control our magnets have over us.

We could argue that every thought, word, and action is

subconsciously driven. How do we separate our externally-generated, subconscious thoughts, words, and actions from the internally-generated, conscious ones? We separate them by examining the reasons underlying them. When we consciously agree with the reasons beneath our decisions and follow through with them, we make conscious choices. When we consciously disagree with the underlying reasons and still follow through with the decision, our subconscious programming controls us.

Demagnetizing Our Magnets
How do we remove the power our subconscious programming has over us and allow ourself to consciously choose the life we want? We demagnetize our magnets in three steps. First, we identify the governing energies that keep us from living the life we consciously want to live. Second, we trace these restraining forces to their origin. Third, we mentally and emotionally give these limiting aspects of ourself back to their original sources.

We identify the limitations we inherited from our past programming by looking at our current life. What about our life today is not the way we want it to be? What part of our governing energies creates this reality? If we are not in the physical condition we want to be in, perhaps it is because we believe this is what we "should" weigh. Our finances, career, or relationships may not be what we want them to be because we subconsciously value and desire our current lifestyle. Our emotions may keep us from experiencing the life we really want. When we identify our governing energies, we see why we have our current personal life, relationships, and career.

Once we identify the specific reasons that led to our current situations, we locate where we learned these values, beliefs, and emotions. We may have perceived our parents telling us that these events would occur. Perhaps we saw their

Magnets

marriage this way and feel this is the way all marriages exist. A certain teacher could have implied we were lazy or stupid, and we held onto this label. Our grade school and high school peers helped create our self-fulfilling prophecy by calling us a jock, brain, nerd, druggie, or brownnoser.

When we connect the reasons for our current situations with the people who directly or indirectly gave us these ideas, we realize these are not our limitations. These beliefs and values represent the limitations we feel other people see in us. We have falsely engrained these ideas into our spirit as if they were originally our own. If we perceive the media telling us we live in a crime-ridden, hopeless, uncaring world with no chance for success or happiness, we don't have to keep on accepting these beliefs. If our role models lacked in self-confidence and we adopted this characteristic, we don't have to continue living by their value system. We give these limitations back to the people who gave them to us by mentally saying,"Thank you very much, but I've decided I don't want these limitations. I am giving them back to you." When we sincerely do this, we remove the power from our magnetic sources.

When we demagnetize our magnets and attain this inner freedom, we go through a frightening experience. Without a subconscious idea of what we should be accomplishing, we find ourself in a world without comfort zones. Fortunately, we simultaneously allow ourself to reach toward our true potential. Rather than returning to some externally programmed ideas of what we will achieve, we consciously choose the spirit we want to center our life around.

What magnets are keeping you from living the life you want? Who originally put these limiting thoughts in your mind? When will you give them back?

Balance

We maintain control over our life by balancing our internal dimensions and external roles.

I really enjoyed playing on see-saws when I was a child. I liked the steady rhythm of going up and down and "working" with a friend to keep the see-saw moving. I did not enjoy riding the see-saw with an older person because they kept me stuck up in the air.

Our life works in the same way. We experience harmony when we balance our internal and external aspects. We balance our internal dimensions by consistently developing our spirit, mind, personality, and body. We balance our external roles by regularly examining and improving our personal life, relationships, and career. We face a wide array of responsibilities in trying to continually improve our internal and external aspects. If we neglect one area, it will eventually dominate all the others for our attention. When we lose our balance, we remain "stuck up in the air". Instead of leading a significant life, we spend our time and energy on these neglected responsibilities. We maintain this internal and external harmony by simplifying our life and staying focused on improving both our internal dimensions and external roles.

What areas of your life seem out of balance? How will you simplify your activities and bring these areas back into balance?

Rules of Reality

Rules of reality exist regardless of how much we develop our human spirit.

We only achieve significance while living in reality. We cannot build our own planet, breed people who do exactly what we want them to do, or contol the weather. The more we understand reality, the more effectively we function within it.

Some Rules of Reality

We never control another person. Even if we set expectations, explain consequences, and enforce these consequences, we can't make someone do something they don't want to do. Conversely, no one controls us. Even though we have to deal with the consequences, we always make our own decisions.

We do not always know what other people are really like. Some people will say one thing and do another. Some people will keep their promises and others won't. People change over time. Their values, principles, and desires change. People commit horrible acts of violence and hatred and incredible acts of caring and kindness every day.

We are not always the person we think we are. We say we believe in something, but our actions tell us a very different story. We change over time. What we stood for ten years ago may not be what we stand for today or ten years from now.

Our relationships are not guaranteed to last a lifetime. We stay close to our friends for forty years or drift apart after a few. Our marriages last until we die or end in divorce. Parents turn on their children and children turn on their parents. Parents love their children and children love their parents. Siblings get angry and never talk to each other again. Siblings grow closer as they grow older. All of these possibilities exist within reality.

People work very hard for a long time, do an excellent

Rules of Reality

job, enhance their organization, and never hear appreciation or get a promotion. In other cases, these people will be treated with dignity, respect, and financial rewards.

People die at the peak of their careers. People die when they are thirty-five years old and have four small children at home. Earthquakes, floods, tornadoes, and volcanos devastate whole communities. People kill other people. Teenagers kill people. Adults kill people. Senior citizens kill people. Cancer, heart attacks, and AIDS kill people of all ages, races, and genders. People lose hope and move through each day in a "living death".

People carefully choose their essence and experience a purposeful life. People overcome natural disasters and man-made catastrophes along the way to achieving their unique desires. People enhance other people's lives. People care deeply about other human beings.

Our health is not guaranteed forever. If we eat fattening food and refuse to exercise, we become fat. If we eat properly and work out regularly, we achieve better physical condition.

The media selects a fragment of reality to focus on and centers their newscasts, magazines, and newspapers around it. This fragment does not represent the complete array of values, beliefs, principles, desires, and emotions in our society.

Words have no meaning without specific definitions. What we say means different things to different people. Only when we explain what our words mean will another person understand us. Only when we understand what certain words mean to another person will we understand them.

If we use up our energy trying to change reality, we lessen our impact within it. By raising our awareness of the rules of reality, we increase our ability to operate effectively within it.

When do you waste energy resisting reality?

Strengthening Our Own Human Spirit

This section contains ideas on identifying our human spirit, letting go of our limiting aspects, purifying our internal dimensions, strengthening our less developed areas, and trusting in a power higher than ourself.

Identifying Our Core

Our core represents the current state of our human spirit.

We begin strengthening our human spirit by identifying the influential events and people from our past and the person we are today.

Recalling Our Influences

Two primary forces shaped our spirit: the people who touched our life in a meaningful way and the important events we experienced. Core People are the family members, friends, mentors, and heroes who have greatly impacted our essence and emotions. Core Experiences helped shape our outlook on life. Through these special situations, we learned particular principles, etched certain values in our mind, and concentrated on new desires.

We learn from our Core Victories by focusing on what led to our success. What obstacles did we overcome? How did we keep going in the face of adversity? What problem-solving methods did we use? What principles, beliefs, and emotions directed our decisions? How did we feel when we finally succeeded? We decipher our success principles for future challenges by examining these victories. We also learn about ourself by examining our Core Failures, the challenges we didn't accept because we didn't want to push beyond our comfort zones. Why did we doubt ourself? What lessons did we learn as a result of stopping?

We remember Core People and Experiences by "speaking" with the person we were at a certain age. How did we at ten years old feel about money? What careers were important to us? What did we want to accomplish with our talents? This thought process requires a dramatic shift in orientation. We gain a whole new perspective by stating what we actually felt when we

Identifying Our Core

were ten years old. After we say what we valued, believed, and desired as a ten-year-old, we explain which friends, teachers, family members, and experiences taught us these ideas. When we give this exercise enough time, we recall an incredible number of significant people and experiences from our past. After we finish, we hold conversations with the person we were at fifteen, twenty, thirty, and forty years old. Through these internal conversations, we see what shaped us into who we are today.

We explain the lessons we learned from important people and events by writing the script for a motion picture about our life. We relive our past by imagining ourself as a talk show guest and answering the questions,"What was the most influential event in your lifetime?" and "Who influenced your life more than any other person?" We learn about ourself by writing our autobiography. Maybe no one else buys it. So what? The stories we select tell us more than they tell the reader. We visualize the essence we received from every member of our family by mentally asking one "value-oriented" or "belief-oriented" question at a time and listening for each individual's answer. Our subconscious mind delivers the message it feels we learned from each person.

Uncovering Our Spirit

Who have we become? Notice the question does not say, "Who do we think we are?", nor "Who would we rather be?" The question is,"Who are we right now?"

We understand who we are by identifying the governing energies that currently guide our decisions. We think we know what we value and believe, but our true spirit could be covered under misperceptions. Since all of our thoughts, words, and actions find their roots in our spirit, we use them as indicators of the governing energies that really drive us.

What thoughts dominate our day? Do we think cynical,

Identifying Our Core

sarcastic, and judgmental thoughts, or do we seek to understand new ideas? What values and beliefs do our current thoughts reflect? Do we value finding the good or weakness in another person? Do we believe the world is a place where we will accomplish our objectives, or do we believe it's impossible to create the destiny we want. When do we feel happiest? saddest? most enthusiastic? most depressed? most interested?

What kinds of statements do we make on a regular basis? Do we communicate messages of hope or hopelessness? What underlying reasons guide our words? Are these reasons consciously or subconsciously driven? What do they tell us about our underlying emotions? Do our most often used statements reflect an underlying frustration or enthusiasm?

What kinds of actions dominate our day? What types of food and how much of it do we actually eat? Do we see food as a reward for working hard, a social centerpiece around which good times revolve, or fuel for our body? What do we read and why? What principles and desires lead us to the books, magazines, and parts of the newspaper we read? What films and television shows do we watch and why do we watch them? How do we use our sexual energy? Why do we use it in this way?

Our external life reflects our internal development. What do our personal life, relationships, and career tell us about our essence? Are we fit or fat? Why do we care for our body the way wo do? What percentage of our income do we save each month? How often do we relax? Do we listen closely to our spouse, boyfriend, or girlfriend or do we discard them with an "uh, huh"? Do we consistently find ourself in abusive relationships or loving, caring relationships? Do we value the sports page more than other people? Do we primarily base our relationships on fulfilling our sexual desires, enhancing our career, or caring for one another? Is our career primarily to help others, to pour our talents toward a meaningful purpose, or to make money? Did we choose

Identifying Our Core

the career we currently have because other people encouraged us to take it or because we valued this type of work?

Our Core Assets help us build the life we want. What aspects of our spirit do we rely on to help us reach our objectives? Perhaps we consider enthusiasm, perseverance, or patience to be our assets. What do we see as our mental assets? Some people see their logical thinking as an asset while others rely on their intuition. What personality assets do we have? Some people see their willingness to listen patiently as their strong suit while others feel confident in being open and honest. What physical assets do we have? How about our eyes? How much time do we save by seeing what is in front of us? How about our ears? Our ability to hear continually provides us with new ideas. What about our arms and legs? How much would we pay to replace them if they were torn off in a tragic accident?

We uncover a great deal of information about our spirit by locating our specific pains and pleasures. Does committing to a long-term relationship cause us pain or pleasure? Does a one night stand cause us pain or pleasure? Our answers provide us with insight into what we value and believe with regard to relationships. Does the idea of working for a very large, well-known company fill us with pain or pleasure? Does the idea of working for ourself fill us with pain or pleasure? Our answers give us an idea of how we perceive security and autonomy.

What questions do we currently ask ourself? We only go after what we ask for. The questions we choose reflect what we value and desire. If we ask,"How will I show my spouse how much he or she means to me?", we demonstrate one type of essence. If we ask,"How will I get my spouse to do what I want him or her to do?", we display another set of values, principles, beliefs, and desires.

We subconsciously or consciously want to be, do, and have certain goals. These objectives rise up from our governing

Identifying Our Core

energies. We locate these Core Dreams by mentally eliminating all of our possible restrictions. What would we be, do, and have if we didn't have any time limits or money restraints and no other person could stop us? How would we care for ourself? What kind of personality would we have? What would our relationships with our family and friends be like? What level of physical fitness would we maintain? What topics would we learn about? What ideas would we share with other people? Where would we travel? What would we do on these trips? Where would we live? What would our house be like? What car would we drive? If we could meet anyone on the planet, who would we talk to? What politicians, athletes, musicians, authors, and movie stars would we discuss ideas with? What would we do for our hobbies? What books would we read? What books would we write? What songs would we compose? What career would we take up? What would we do for other people? What diseases would we cure? What prejudices would we break down? After we write down our Core Dreams, we identify the governing energies which led to them by asking, "Why do I have each of these Core Dreams?" Our answers reveal our true spirit.

What did you learn from the Core People and Experiences in your life? How would you describe your spirit today?

Releasing Our Balloons

Our balloons keep us from living the life we consciously want to live.

We see our balloons and the reasons for releasing them by imagining a track star getting in position for the one hundred meter dash. This particular athlete has several Olympic gold medals, years of experience, and tremendous inner faith. The starter's gun goes off. Pow! This star sprinter gallops across the finish line in first place. In the very next race, this same runner has water balloons tied onto his wrists, stomach, thighs, calves, and ankles. These water balloons are so strong they won't break when they hit the runner or the ground. The starter's gun goes off. Pow! When this outstanding veteran takes off, the water balloons start bouncing around and into each other. The athlete trips and falls to the ground. With great perseverance, this sprinter gets up and tries to run again. The balloons start flying around and bring this person down again. After two more attempts, this experienced and successful athlete gives up. He realizes he must release the balloons before he will succeed.

The same principle holds for us. During our lifetime, we develop strong qualities and strive to achieve meaningful goals. We also tie several "balloons" onto our human spirit. Our balloons waste our time, drain our energy, block our intuition, and restrict us from living the life we consiously want. We enhance our ability to achieve our goals by releasing our balloons.

Seeing Our Balloons

Our balloons reside within us. Another person does not represent one of our balloons because they exist outside of us. Negative feelings about the person do represent a balloon. We tie a balloon onto our spirit when we automatically follow or rebel against their criticisms. If we do things only to receive praise, we give up the life we really want. When we stay with the group's

Releasing Our Balloons

decisions only to avoid ostracization, we relinquish our ability to achieve significance. If we react in a predictable manner to certain statements, tones of voice, or facial expressions, we allow the other person's personality to control us. If we change what we stand for every time we interact with a person in a different role, we forfeit the experiences we desire.

When we allow tangible items to interfere with what we consciously value, we turn them into balloons. If our desire for a particular house, car, or type of food grows stronger than our desire to stand for what we believe in, we center our efforts around these externals. Heavy traffic, overcrowded rooms, dirty living environments, and loud noises do not force a bad mood into us. We create our moods by the way we respond to these tangible situations.

A flood, storm, fire, or earthquake alters the way we view life if we let it. We tie another balloon on when we allow a disaster to convince us to quit trying.

When we live to attain a particular number, we lose touch with our internal essence. We live in a society consumed with numbers. We rank ourselves by our weight, salary, and the number of people who report to us. We transform these numbers into balloons by valuing them more than the development of our mind, body, and personality.

We contain many of our restrictive forces in our emotions. If shame, regret, worry, guilt, fear, anger, frustration, and stress flow through us, they halt our achievements. These feelings often rise up from a variety of childhood issues. Unless we work through these issues, we remain stuck in a restrictive frame of mind. If worry and fear dominate our spirit, we ignore our true desires. When we compare ourself to others, we feel embarrassed, doubt our abilities, or experience a false sense of superiority.

Our obsessions drain away many of our creative

Releasing Our Balloons

energies. When we compulsively think about our achievements, embarrassing moments, future opportunities, new clothes, or physical attractiveness, we throw our internal and external life out of balance. We turn them into balloons by spending too much time and effort on any one of them.

Releasing Our Balloons

By raising our level of self-awareness, we begin the process of releasing a particular balloon. When we realize our obsessions with drugs, alcohol, chocolate, or complaining, we endure a great deal of pain. If we never face the darkness, the subconsciously controlled world of magnets and balloons, we never move into the light, the life we consciously want to live. When we see our balloons, we start to make plans for letting go of them. If materialism controls us, we begin releasing it by realizing the control it has over us. Our childhood experiences frequently determine our decisions, but we won't resolve these issues until we raise our awareness of them. We step toward releasing our balloons by moving into the "comfort zone/non-comfort zone cycle". When we do something often enough, we turn it into a comfort zone. We don't enjoy our friends ridiculing us, but we sometimes go back for more. We don't enjoy weighing twenty-five pounds more than we desire, but sometimes we shove more food into our mouth than our body can handle. We do these things because we have done them for so long that we have turned them into comfort zones. We break these comfort zones by becoming aware of them. When we realize that we let our friends ridicule us and we eat poorly, we feel uncomfortable. We want to return to these old ways, but we can't comfortably go back with this new level of self-awareness. We create new comfort zones by letting go of these habits and selecting relationships and food that we feel comfortable with.

We further release our balloons by accepting them as

Releasing Our Balloons

part of our core. When we deny having them, they control us. If we see our balloons as reality, we take steps to resolve them. We accept ourself with all of our unique characteristics by accepting other people with all of their facial expressions, idiosyncracies, and attitudes. By accepting other people and ourself as we are right now, we release the balloons of criticizing others and worrying about what they think of us.

We release the power our restraining emotions have over us by experiencing and expressing them. If we feel angry toward another person and refuse to express it, this emotion festers inside of us. Our anger grows larger and larger until it dominates the rest of our governing energies. If, instead of holding onto our anger, we write them a letter or discuss our feelings with them, we diminish the long-term effect our anger has over us.

We sometimes focus on attaining a particular result to the point we give our self-control over to the goal. We allow the goal to get what it wants out of us. We see ourself as a "failure" if we don't achieve our desires. We release this balloon by understanding the importance of the process. Every result we achieve comes about because of the process we used. If the result does not satisfy us, we keep changing the process until it does. Our focus moves from "failed result" to "improving the process". This shift in perspective allows us to redefine success and failure. Rather than defining success as, "Achieving a meaningful goal", we redefine it as, "Striving toward the attainment of a meaningful goal." Instead of failure meaning, "Not achieving our meaningful goals", we redefine it as, "Not trying to achieve our meaningful goals". When we detach ourself from the results we desire and focus on the process of achievement, we release the balloons of inadequacy, fear, and stress.

The principle of "thought expansion" means, "Whatever we think about expands." If we cause a balloon to grow larger by

Releasing Our Balloons

focusing on the thing we don't want, we release this balloon by concentrating on the things we do want. The more we think about what we really want, the more we create these results.

When we forgive past actions, we release the control these deeds have over us. We may have said the wrong thing, tried to start up our own business and ended up losing a great deal of money, or gone on a diet only to end up weighing more than when we started. Another person may have insulted us or lied to us. As a result, we sometimes decide to never trust ourself or other people again. This "stop trusting" mentality eliminates many of the possible achievements we desire. When we forgive, we decrease the power our past has over us and increase the power we have over our future. If we don't forgive, we emotionally carry these actions with us for a very long time. The accumulated weight of all these past deeds pulls us down.

When we honestly communicate with another person, we discuss the issues straining our relationship and release their negative effect. This type of discussion requires both empathetic listening and honest expression of our thoughts and feelings. When we honestly communicate with ourself, we reflect on the internal issues keeping us from living the life we consciously want to live. Our internal discussion requires some degree of quiet in order to hear our spirit.

We release our balloons by reducing the complexities of our personal life, relationships, and career. As we simplify our material needs, living environment, relationship expectations, and career desires, we reduce the pressure we place on ourself. When we unclutter our mind, we see more clearly what principles, values, beliefs, and desires we want to base our decisions on.

Sometimes our balloons grow so large, we can't consciously release them. We feel powerless versus them. By listening to a divine higher power and acting on what we hear, we begin to regain control of our life. When we have faith in a higher

Releasing Our Balloons

power, we no longer need to face our challenges alone. We step forward with renewed strength.

What balloons keep you from living the life you consciously desire? How will you release them?

Purifying Our System

We reach higher levels of development by purifying our human spirit.

Purifying Our Human Spirit

Whatever we put into a system eventually comes back out. We strengthen our human spirit by carefully selecting what we pour into our spirit, mind, body, and personality.

We purify our spirit by deliberately choosing the essence we feel will help us reach our highest level. We become what we believe in, value, and desire. We strengthen our emotional state by emphasizing our enriching emotions. When we use our positive emotions of joy, happiness, and enthusiasm, they play a major role in our development.

We become what we think about. We think about what we put into our mind. We determine our future by carefully choosing what we pour into our mind. We purify our mind by consciously selecting the books, tapes, magazines, films, television shows, newspapers, and conversations we feed into it. Without new ideas to challenge, change, and reinforce our old ideas, we limit our personal growth.

We purify our personality by dedicating ourself to our relationships rather than seeing them as obstacles to our objectives. We improve our personality by extending large amounts of commitment, empathetic listening, and honesty to the people we interact with. Our personality improves when we truly care about other people and stop doing things to control or manipulate them.

We purify our physical dimension by carefully selecting what we eat and drink, how often we exercise and how we exercise, and the amount of rest and relaxation we receive.

How will you purify and strengthen the dimensions of your human spirit?

Completing Our Core

We complete our core by strengthening the less developed aspects of our human spirit.

Just as a chain can only pull the weight that its weakest link will handle, we can only achieve what the weakest aspect of our human spirit will handle. Any part of ourself that we refuse to enhance holds us back from living the life we consciously want.

Identifying and Strengthening
Our Weakest Aspects

When we describe what we see as our major characteristics, we indirectly describe our less developed aspects. If we see ourself as a hardworking, focused, and project-oriented individual, we describe our strengths and our less developed areas. What do we feel we need to strengthen? In this case, our weaknesses may include not relaxing enough and needing to invest more time in our relationships. Do we personally want greater honesty in expressing our true emotions or greater assertiveness in telling our ideas? Do we feel we need to project more tenderness or toughness? Should we provide more compassion, sensitivity, nurturing, and caring or more aggressive, solution-oriented, problem-solving actions?

We strengthen our less developed areas through affirmations. If we see ourself as a purely rational thinker, we say,"I cherish my instincts and follow through with what they tell me." If we see ourself only as a good listener, we complete our core by saying,"I cherish my opinion and willingly share my thoughts with other people."

Which time frame do we live in right now? If we always live in the past, present, or future, we close off the other perspectives. We complete our core by viewing life from each of these frames of reference. By mentally going back five years in the past, we see if we have evolved into the person we wanted to

Completing Our Core

become. What would we leave the same? What would we change? Five years from now, what kind of person do we want to be? Are we currently making decisions that will make this vision of the future a reality? When we mentally integrate the past, present, and future, we take responsibility for all of them.

If we listen exclusively to our inner child, inner adolescent, or inner adult, we shove the others into our subconscious mind. The voices we ignore will leap out at us when we least expect them. While we interact with our boss, we will act sarcastically and rebelliously. While socializing with our friends, we will dominate the discussion and demand attention. We integrate these three aspects of our spirit by writing our autobiography. We start by going as far back in our childhood as we can remember. By sinking deeper and deeper into the feelings we experienced as a child, we mentally and emotionally relive these years. We re-experience our adolescence by remembering the times we questioned our parents' rationale, expressed our ideas to other people, and kept our feelings trapped inside of us. We visualize ourself as an adult by remembering when we took responsibility for a situation and tried to stay on top of things. By combining the wonder of childhood, the independence of adolescence, and the responsibility of adulthood, we strengthen our spirit.

We sometimes experience internal chaos between our spirituality and sexuality. Objectives we intuitively receive from a higher power often conflict with our sexual desires and cause us to experience frustration and guilt. We resolve this problem by synergizing these two energies. We realize the beauty and power of our sexual energy and direct it toward enriching our personal development, relationships, and life's main purpose.

Mirrors don't lie. When we look into a mirror, we see our physical body exactly as it is at that moment. Whether we feel really good or really bad about what we see, the mirror merely reflects reality back to us. The mirror is neither good nor bad. If we're not happy with what we see, we either complain about how life is unfair or we work to get in better condition. Our personality, finances, relationships, career, and hobbies also serve as our mirrors. They reflect information to us about our reality. We use this information to complete our core.

When we judge or criticize someone else, we may be criticizing ourself for the very same reason. If we criticize someone for being too loud at social gatherings, this person represents a mirror for us. They send out a tremendous amount of information, but we only pick up on their loudness. Perhaps we isolate this characteristic because we subconsciously see it as one of our weaknesses. The things we find fault with in another person tell us a great deal about us. This type of mirror reflects back to us what we do have and don't want.

We may criticize some aspect of another person's personality because we lack this characteristic. This type of mirror tells us what we don't have and do want. We sometimes see other people doing what they believe is the right thing to do and sarcastically call them "Little Miss Perfect", "Mr. Positive", or "a big phony". We admire their integrity and criticize them because we are jealous. By understanding this mirror, we let go of the need to judge others and shift this energy toward attaining the traits we desire.

If we go below another person's action or statement and examine the underlying value, belief, principle, or desire, we learn more about ourself. If we interact with a salesperson and find out he lied to us, we feel extremely angry and want to scream at him. What disturbed us so deeply? The salesperson acted concerned and understanding. This person didn't verbally or physically abuse us. Yet, we wanted to tear him to shreds. Why? We felt this person displayed a lack of integrity. Through the principle of mirroring, we see personal integrity as an important

Completing Our Core

issue within us. We may feel a need to strengthen our own integrity.

Sometimes other people criticize us because our action reflects something within them. Their criticism may tell us they either do the same thing and want to stop or they wish they did it. Other people's criticisms often describe their weaknesses more than ours.

We may see our work as an unimportant activity. We feel a more meaningul job would make our life more purposeful. Our perspective toward our career mirrors the way we see ourself. By finding a purpose in our current line of work, we feel more purposeful as individuals.

Aches and pains tell us to exercise regularly, relax more often, and stretch our muscles before and after working out. When we spend money recklessly or save every penny we make, our financial mirror reflects one of our missing aspects. We may not feel important unless we spend a great deal of money or save like a miser. If we live in an extremely messy home, our environmental mirror tells us we don't spend enough time caring for ourself. Every aspect of our life reflects information back to us. By increasing our awareness of these mirrors, we realize our less developed aspects and work to develop them.

What are the less developed areas in your life? How will you strengthen them and complete your own core?

Trusting Our Intuition

Our intuition represents the ideas we receive from a divine higher power.

I believe there exists a power greater than our own consciousness. I believe we strengthen our human spirit and strive toward significance by allowing this higher power to influence our spirit and guide our decisions.

Listening To A Higher Power

We listen to this higher power in many different ways. We do this by saying formal prayers, using one or more of many different types of meditation, or asking this higher power for a message and waiting for it to arrive. We improve our ability to hear these divine ideas by slowing down and going into a mentally quiet space. This divine source remains available to us always.

When we surrender the influence our subconscious programming has over us and give it to a higher power, our magnets and balloons still try to pull us down. When we listen to our intuition, we add another tool for overcoming these restraining forces. Trusting our intuition means listening to a higher power and acting on the ideas we hear. As we turn to this divine energy, we increase our level of personal power and enhance our personal development.

We visualize trusting our intuition by imagining ourself as a leaf floating down a river. The leaf does not know where it is going, but it trusts the river to bring it to its unique destination. The leaf doesn't cling to the tree, but willingly participates in the flow of the river. The river represents divine energy. By trusting in this divine energy, we step into the flow of a higher power and move directly to our unique purpose.

When we try to decipher between our subconscious magnets and the voice of a higher power, we make mistakes. We sometimes follow our subconscious limitations without realizing it. With time and practice, we separate the voice of a higher power and any restraining messages from our subconscious programming. In doing so, we take another step toward strengthening our own human spirit.

How will you tap into the wisdom of the higher power within you?

My Story

    I tell my story to help you understand how the philosophy of inside-out living evolved in my life. In addition to my own experiences, I read numerous self-help books and studied successful people. I searched for ideas that would help me achieve a meaningful life. Since I always wanted to know how these authors developed their particular way of thinking, I thought you would want to know how I developed mine.

Personal Journey of Development

Grade School

My family and books influenced me a great deal. I have three older brothers and sisters and two younger ones. I tried to be my own person while subconsciously comparing myself to the others. Looking back now I realize my parents never wanted us to be more than the best we could be. At the time, I felt enormous pressure to outperform my siblings in both academics and athletics. I also read biography after biography. I would go to the library and take out the maximum number of books and read each book in a day or two. I filled my mind with stories of people who stood up for what they believed in and made meaningful contributions to society.

My desire to stand up for what I believed in spilled over into the classroom. Every time one of my male classmates made fun of another student, I stepped in and fought him. I got in fights constantly throughout grade school. I saw myself as the Lone Ranger, Robin Hood, and Thomas Edison all rolled into one. I didn't realize how little I allowed myself to just be me. I acted out the roles I learned in books. As much as I thought I consciously made my own decisions, I really created situations where other people wanted to fight me and make fun of me. Some of my classmates called me "Leader of the Fags" and played a game called "Cough-It-Up-Coughlin" where six or seven other boys would throw big, red, rubber balls at me, and I would fight back. I lived from the outside-in. I wanted to act like my book heroes and stand apart from the others, but I gained terribly low self-confidence because no one seemed to like or respect me. Even when my eighth grade classmates voted me "Most Intelligent", "Most Athletic", and "Most Likely To Succeed", I still saw myself as an ugly kid who had little chance to achieve anything meaningful.

Personal Journey of Development

High School and College

During the next eight years, I swung to the other outside-in extreme. I told myself I never wanted to fight anyone again. No matter what others said or did I refused to argue with them. I would do anything to try to appease others and make them like me. I never displayed anger. I often acted like a clown. I rarely traded serious thoughts with anyone and cracked jokes all the time. I worked extremely hard at my schoolwork in high school to attain impressive grades, but I wanted others to like me at the same time. I thought these were contradictory concepts. I tried so hard to get others to like me that I turned most of them away.

While in high school and college, I achieved a certain degree of external success. I graduated from high school in the top ten percent of my class and played varsity soccer my junior and senior years. I graduated from the University of Notre Dame with a degree in mechanical engineering and lettered twice in soccer. However, I still allowed other people's opinions to control my decisions and the way I perceived myself.

After the soccer season ended my senior year in college, I gained thirty pounds right away. I skipped classes constantly. I told myself I didn't want to participate in the "self-centered and materialistic" mentality of my classmates. In reality, I took the easy way out. I literally quit trying just to "show" others I wouldn't participate in their "selfish" approach to life. I thought the students who were doing well in school only wanted to get good grades so they could get a good job and make a lot of money. By reacting to my false perceptions of others, I once again allowed outside-in thinking to control me. I missed out on a great deal of information by skipping classes and supposedly "standing up for what I believed in".

I decided I didn't want a career as an engineer or as a salesman. I wanted to apply the logical thinking I had learned in college toward an organization. I wanted to teach what I called

Personal Journey of Development

"The Total Team Concept", which meant each member of an organization benefits when everyone strives to help every other member.

College Coaching

From August 1985 to January 1990, I was a collegiate head soccer coach. In some ways, I learned more during these five years than during any other period of my life. In other ways, I view this experience as my codependent years.

In March of my senior year in college, I signed on as the head soccer coach of Tri-State University in Angola, Indiana. I was hired to build a brand new soccer program. From an inside-out perspective, I took a big step toward living the life I consciously wanted by taking this job. Many people thought I was crazy to go into college coaching rather than engineering or sales. I felt I could help people reach their individual and organizational potential by serving as a head coach. I hoped my players would take the ideas of caring for themselves and other people and pour them into their personal lives, relationships, and careers. I believed I could contribute to society in a positive way through this position. In addition to coaching and recruiting, I served as Dorm Director for the largest dormitory on campus. In return, I received three thousand dollars and room and board.

During my first year, I met individually with all eighteen players five times to go over their goals in both academics and athletics. I sent out over eighteen hundred recruiting letters, met with over a hundred recruits on campus, and signed eighteen new players from all over the country to come to Tri-State. In 1986, we went from one win to nine wins and finished second in the state tournament at the end of the year. I was named coach-of-the-year for NAIA (National Association of Intercollegiate Athletics) coaches in the state of Indiana. Early in 1987, I signed on as the head coach of DePaul University. Even though I

54

Personal Journey of Development

experienced external success at this time, I sensed that I was moving away from the reasons why I initially became a head coach. I tried to impress others, but I didn't take care of myself. I still weighed thirty pounds more than when I stopped playing and had no savings in the bank. At both Tri-State and DePaul, I would do almost anything for my players because subconsciously I wanted them to assure me that I was a good person. This attitude eventually ran its course at DePaul.

After teaching high school math for two years in Chicago to supplement my five thousand dollar coaching salary at DePaul, I lost my teaching position because of a sharp decrease in enrollment. The newest teacher in each department was let go. In my final year as a head coach, I made $84 a week and my rent was $475 a month. After the season, I took a position as an assistant janitor for six dollars an hour and as a waiter in a deli for four dollars an hour. Meanwhile, I kept recruiting for new players and meeting with the current ones. I thought the players needed me so badly that I had to stay for them. In reality, I needed the players so badly that I had to stay with them. Whatever small amount of inside-out thinking I had entered college coaching with had now shifted completely to outside-in thinking. The only time I felt I had any self-worth was when I discussed goals with one of my players. Subconsciously, I needed to feel that they depended on me. By January 1990, I had accumulated nearly $3000 of debt on my credit cards. Every day I cleaned out toilets and picked up trash for the people who lived in the same building I lived in. I experienced the final blow when I learned my mother had cancer. I could no longer keep asking my parents for money to support my "dream". My mother recovered from her cancer, but I didn't know she would at that time.

The culmination of these events woke me up. I went to DePaul's athletic director and asked for a raise or another job on campus. When he refused to do either one, I resigned. In my

Personal Journey of Development

three years at DePaul, we won only ten games. It didn't matter to me that we only had six players on the team when I took over and roughly two thousand dollars left for scolarships to recruit with. It didn't matter to me that I had to drive the whole team twenty-five minutes to a practice field with no goals on it. I thought our lack of success was all my fault. I felt as low as I possibly could. From the outside-in, I saw myself as a failure. I was thirty pounds overweight, broke, three thousand dollars in debt, and unemployed. I desperately wanted someone to tell me I was OK. I allowed outside-in thinking to consume me.

I took a job as a headhunter for a professional sales search company in Chicago for the next three months. I thought it was a perfect match for my skills. I "recruited" good salespeople from one company and helped them find "better" jobs with another. I received a commission each time a person took a new job. I felt I was helping individuals and companies become the best they could be while making money doing it. I really felt as though I had found the right medium to coincide with my original reasons for going into coaching. Unfortunately, it didn't turn out that way. Every day I called up various companies and told an assortment of lies to get the names of their salespeople. A few days later, I called these salespeople and told them they were "recommended to me by a very good friend of theirs who would have to remain nameless because of confidential reasons" for an opening at another company. After about two and a half months of doing this, I broke down crying. I knew my life had to have a different purpose. I wanted to help myself and others reach their potential, but I had spent the last five years worrying about winning soccer games, recruiting players, and lying to people to leave their job for a new one. I started with an inside-out approach five years earlier, but I quickly shifted to outside-in and stayed that way for the duration. I was not living the life I consciously wanted to live. My life did not stand for anything. I needed to regroup and try again.

St. Louis

In May 1990, I called the principal of St. Louis University High School and asked him if he needed any teachers in math or science. Two weeks later I had the position I wanted. I came back to St. Louis to teach math and serve as the assistant head varsity soccer coach.

I moved back for several reasons. I needed some stability and a regular paycheck for awhile. I wanted to be part of an environment that challenged people to reach toward their potential and supported them along the way. I wanted to truly educate. The word "educo" means "to draw out". I wanted to help students and players draw out the best they had within them. I wanted balance in my life. I wanted to learn about adult education and how to teach success principles to other people. My personal pendulum started to slowly swing from outside-in to inside-out thinking. I gradually moved toward living the life I consciously desired.

August 6, 1990 was a big day for me. I drove from Chicago to St. Louis and went directly to work out at Bally's Vic Tanny. I started my program for losing the extra thirty pounds I had carried around for five years. From Vic Tanny, I called The Dale Carnegie Institute and asked for information on a course in effective speaking and human relations. A week later, a good friend of mine, Joyce Feder, gave me a copy of Og Mandino's The Greatest Miracle in the World. This book opened my mind. A new era in my life was starting to unfold.

I started reading self-help books at a rapid pace. During the next five years, I purchased and read approximately a hundred and fifty of these books. New ideas replaced old ones. I realized other people felt the same way I did about approaching life from the inside-out. A year after I moved to St. Louis, I turned

Personal Journey of Development

these ideas into a course called "The Self Concept Course" and later "The Adventure of Life Course". I started giving "motivational" talks to various groups around St. Louis. Very slowly and very steadily, I continued shifting my personal orientation from outside-in to inside-out. My self-confidence and self-discipline grew stronger. I learned to take care of myself mentally, physically, emotionally, and spiritually. I learned I could care about others without having to control them. I learned I could express my thoughts and other people wouldn't run away. I started trusting my intuition and listening to God's voice rather than the subconscious voices that were pulling at me to be someone other than who I really am. I started developing more meaningful relationships with my friends, family, and co-workers. Throughout this whole experience, I grew to understand and outline this philosophy of inside-out living. One more turning point awaited me.

The Choice

Even though, in retrospect, the event seems almost trivial, the lessons I learned and the responses I chose had a great influence on me. In April 1993, Ebbie Dunn retired as the head soccer coach of St. Louis University High School after thirty-eight years of service. At that time, I was thirty years old. During my career, I played soccer for sixteen years, served as a head college coach for five years, and was Ebbie Dunn's assistant coach for three years. I very much wanted and expected to be the next head coach. I saw this as the perfect opportunity to do what I had set out to do eight years earlier. Rather than recruiting players, I thought I could focus my energies on helping each individual and the team as a whole reach their highest potential. Within the framework of the team, I could help each person implement his own personality and talents toward a common cause. I felt completely prepared for

Personal Journey of Development

the challenge. I was experienced and enthusiastic. However, the three member board selected another teacher for the position. They told me I was too naive. They said they didn't believe I would do what I said I would do. I felt devastated. I thought this was the opportunity I had been preparing for during the previous eight years. In reality, this event served as the catalyst I needed to go further within myself and consciously decide what I wanted my life to stand for.

During the next two months, I felt angry, frustrated, and cheated out of a position I knew I could do well. I thought I would never get a chance to prove myself as a success. These feelings caused me to see my true self. I realized how outside-in thinking still controlled my spirit. I allowed other people's decisions to affect my self-esteem and emotions. I focused on losing the title of "head coach" rather than finding new ways to help myself and other people reach toward our highest potential. When I realized what I was doing, I reread Og Mandino's <u>The Greatest Miracle in the World</u>. I read "The God Memorandum" from that book over and over again. I concentrated on what I had going for myself and how I could help other people. I examined my values, beliefs, principles, and desires. I decided to stop waiting for the perfect position to come along and start working to create my own career. I decided I would spend as much time as was necessary to derive the success principles I would base my life on. I started reading more books on living consciously and letting go of the subconscious voices that continually pulled at me. I studied various twelve-step programs and learned about codependency. Rather than trying to slide these principles in during a math class or soccer practice, I decided I would someday teach them directly through books, speeches, seminars, and consulting. I began to write this book the summer after the coaching decision was made.

I did not have a choice as to who was named the next

Personal Journey of Development

head coach. I did have a choice as to how I would respond to their decision. I'm proud to say I used this experience as another step toward reaching my ultimate goal of helping myself and other people live the lives we consciously want to live. Through learning, implementing, and teaching this philosophy of inside-out thinking, I believe I am leading a significant life. After ten years of searching, I finally realized this is the only goal I ever really wanted to achieve.

What is the story of your journey of development?

INITIATIVE

Stepping Out

The next eight chapters contain fundamental principles for helping us achieve our goals. This section begins with a system for consciously selecting a purpose and creating a plan for reaching it. The ensuing chapters include ideas on:

visualizing our completed objectives

developing habits that enhance our chances for success

solving the problems we encounter

strengthening our mental approach

reinforcing our spirit

maintaining the successful completion of our goals

expanding the areas in which we set our goals.

As we apply these principles in real-life situations, we step further into the light of conscious living.

Quality Questions

We increase the quality of our life by asking questions and searching for the answers.

Every goal we set requires a purpose and a process for reaching this purpose. This connection between purpose and process acts as the operating mechanism for increasing the quality of our lives. Quality is not the end product or the process of creating the end-product. Quality connects the two. We join these two components by answering specific questions.

Purpose Questions

In order to make a dream come true, we must first have the dream. This cliche seems overwhelmingly obvious, but we waste time and energy when we do not identify our purpose before getting into action. By choosing a specific objective and the reasons for having it, we direct our internal resources toward accomplishing it. The first quality question is,

"What is my purpose and why do I want to achieve it?"

If we establish a goal and find no valid reasons for going after it, we drop this as one of our objectives. If we establish a goal and find several valid reasons for pursuing it, we gain motivation for reaching it.

Process Questions

We develop our plan of action for achieving this purpose by answering a series of questions.

"How will I accomplish this goal?"

We write out the steps we will take to achieve our goal. These steps serve as a foundation for future evaluations. After we take action, we reflect on our gameplan and look for ways to improve it. We use an alternative method for reaching our goal when we follow through on our instincts. Even if our decision

Quality Questions

does not seem logical, it may help us reach our objective in the long run.

"What Core Assets will I use to achieve this purpose?"

In answering this question, we turn our attention inward and focus on our strengths rather than our weaknesses.

"When will I work toward and achieve this goal?"

When we commit the pursuit of our goal to a timetable, we make it part of our daily pattern.

"Where will this goal take place?"

We enhance our chances of reaching our goal by imagining the environment where it will take place.

"Who will I work with toward reaching this goal?"

As we carefully share our goal with people who support our efforts, we increase our motivation.

"What problems will I encounter as I move toward achieving this goal?"

We take the first step toward solving a problem by identifying it. We locate our problem by using the concept of cause and effect. When we encounter a problem, we trace it to a particular cause. This particular cause may be the effect of another cause. We work our way backwards until we identify the specific underlying cause that keeps us from accomplishing our goal. This underlying cause may be one of our values, beliefs, principles, desires, or emotions. After we identify the root cause keeping us from reaching our objective, we effectively weed the problem out. The chapter on "Problem Solvers" has ideas for actually solving our problems.

How would you answer each of the quality questions for your most important objectives?

Future Realities

We create future realities by imagining we have already achieved our objectives.

When Carib Martin, an architect out of Pratt Institute, designs a building, he sees himself walking through every room before the foundation has been laid. He points out,"The house is a reality. It is not a physical reality, but it is a reality in my mind. In the physical world, the house is a future reality. Once I design it, I am convinced I will build it." By using this method, we convince ourself that we will achieve our objectives.

Consciously Constructing The Future

We deliberately control our imagination by fantasizing about our desires. We raise our level of faith through vivid, detailed, and exciting daydreams. When we make our daydreams specific and real, we increase our chances for achieving them. We enhance our daydreams by relaxing, fixing the desired image in our mind, fueling it with positive thoughts, and allowing the energy of a higher power to flow through it.

"Future reality environments" convince us that we have already succeeded. If we want to vacation in a particular location, we make it seem as though we just returned from there. We write postcards stating what a great time we had, put "souvenirs" in our living room for safekeeping, write a journal of all the places we "saw" and all the people we "met", and get together with friends to "relive" the trip. If we want a career as a doctor, we create a future reality environment by hanging a white doctor's coat up in our room, making a nameplate with our name on it and the initials M.D. after it, and placing a medical diploma over our desk. If we want to operate our own business someday, we print stationary with our fictitious company's logo on it, store our future client list in a computer, and place our mission statement on the wall.

We enhance our future realities by actually living our

Future Realities

dream on a small scale. If we wish to be a lawyer, we volunteer to assist at a law firm. If the idea of selling intrigues us, we sell raffle tickets for a local charity. If we dream of being a major college basketball coach, we volunteer to coach a grade school team.

We create future realities through affirmations. By filling in the statement, "I am _____" with words describing what we want, we speak as though our dreams have already come true. "I am happy, I am healthy, I am happily married, I am wealthy, I am doing what I've always wanted." We will not magically perform beyond our capacities by using this technique, but we will reach much closer to our potential.

By going through our photo albums, we mentally return to our college graduation, first job, and wedding day. We see our parents and friends in situations we forgot about a long time ago. We "relive" our future accomplishments by making a photo album of the car, house, and career we desire. We insert future newspaper articles about the impact we "had" on the community around us. We toss in future letters from friends congratulating us on our achievements and thanking us for caring about them.

Other people help us create our future realities. If we desire a special house, workplace, or retreat center, we hire an architect to design this building exactly the way we want it. We enhance the faith we have in ourself by associating with supportive and successful people. People who continually point out our best assets represent a valuable resource for helping us achieve our objectives. When we surround ourself with people who strengthen our internal reality, we enhance our ability to achieve the external reality we want.

How will you make your most meaningful goal seem as though it has already been achieved?

Creating Quality Habits

Quality habits help us reach our objectives.

If we want sunlight to go through a forest of trees and hit the grass, we do one of three things. We attain a short-term solution by cutting off the leaves. We reach longer lasting results by chopping the trees down. We achieve lasting success by digging the trees out by their roots and allowing the sun to continually light up the grass. We use three similar methods in changing poor habits into positive ones.

Cutting The Leaves

We begin by identifying our purpose. For example, we may want to eat fruits and vegetables instead of ice cream. After we clarify our purpose, we summarize the beneficial reasons for changing: greater physical condition, larger reservoirs of energy, and enhanced self-esteem. We also associate ridiculous amounts of pain with our negative habit. We imagine three gallons of ice cream pouring into our throat and choking us while more ice cream falls on our head and starts suffocating us. After this, we use patternbreakers to shift our concentration from the subconscious to the conscious. When we desire ice cream, our desire begins subconsciously. When we drive home from work, we get a craving for ice cream and stop at the grocery store. We control this decision by making it a conscious one. We use a patternbreaker by shouting over and over again,"I'm free of ice cream at last!" This patternbreaker forces us to consciously choose between buying ice cream and doing something else. At this point, we focus on the extraordinary pain we associated with eating ice cream and the pleasurable reasons we associated with eating fruits and vegetables. After reviewing our reasons, we choose the fruits and vegetables and eat them. We develop a new habit by repeating this process over and over.

When we use this method for creating quality habits, we

change our habits very rapidly. We do face some problems with this method. Because it bypasses our internal essence, we do not make any conscious connection with our values, beliefs, and principles. We temporarily trick our mind into hating ice cream and loving fruits and vegetables. This trick eventually wears off if we do not internalize this new way of thinking.

Chopping At The Trunk

We create longer lasting habits by imagining two circles with the words "Intention" and "Attention" written on each of them.

The first circle refers to subconscious living. It has the word "Attention" written across the top and the word "Intention" written across the bottom. We subconsciously pay attention to what other people put in front of us and allow them to choose our intentions.

Subconscious Living

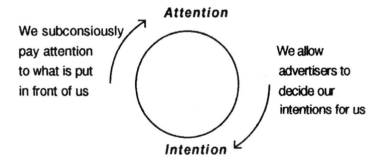

Attention

We subconsiously pay attention to what is put in front of us

We allow advertisers to decide our intentions for us

Intention

The second circle refers to conscious living. It has the word "Intention" written across the top of the circle and the word

Creating Quality Habits

"Attention" written across the bottom. We consciously choose our intentions and pay attention to externals fitting in with these intentions.

Conscious Living

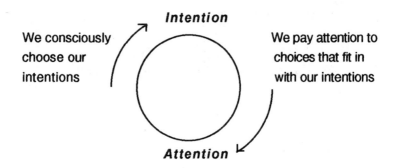

We apply these principles to our eating example in the following manner. If we don't consciously choose what we eat, we place ourself on the first circle. From this perspective, we invest attention in what the advertising world and our friends put in front of us. Advertisements for Dairy Queen and Baskin-Robbins quickly fill our mind. We subconsciously focus our intention on eating ice cream. We create quality habits by placing ourself on the second circle and consciously choosing our intentions. If we decide to eat fruits and vegetables rather than ice cream, we narrow our focus considerably. As we move around the circle, we pay attention to advertisements concerning fruits and vegetables, and we eat fruits and vegetables.

Even though this method works effectively for longer periods of time than the first method, the "Intention-Attention Circle" loses its effectiveness when we feel overly tired. If we

Creating Quality Habits

don't have the necessary energy to maintain our conscious approach to eating, the external world will decide for us what we subconsciously invest attention in. This pattern will snowball until we lose conscious control of our decisions.

Digging Up The Roots

When we make a decision, we follow some internal reason. We uncover the hidden aspects of our essence by examining our poor habits. After we identify the specific values, beliefs, principles, or desires causing these habits, we change these patterns by choosing different governing energies. With the ice cream example, we identify the specific aspect of our essence that leads us to eating ice cream in the first place. What particular values, principles, desires, or beliefs do we implement when we eat ice cream? Perhaps when we grew up our family sat around the kitchen table after dinner and ate ice cream. As a result, we subconsciously associate eating ice cream with the value of family togetherness, belief in caring for other people, principle of respecting others, and desire to be with people close to our hearts. In our childhood, our parents may have rewarded us with ice cream for doing a good job. Today, we subconsciously connect rewarding ourself with eating ice cream. After we see how this action grows out of our essence, we make specific internal changes. We realize eating ice cream has less to do with rewards and togetherness and more to do with gaining weight and feeling listless. We value fruits and vegetables for the health and energy they bring us. We believe in the long-term benefits of eating fruits and vegetables for our heart. As we shift our controlling energies, we change our corresponding decisions and create life-long, quality habits.

What habits would you like to change? How will you change them?

Problem Solvers

Problem Solvers attack the issues keeping us from our objectives.

We over say the phrase "Have a positive mental attitude", but we never over use the principle. When we use a positive attitude, we focus on finding the possibility for success within the problem. Problems are the obstacles we need to work through to achieve what we want. Problems contain opportunities for personal growth. When we have a positive attitude, we search for the aspect of the problem that helps us grow.

We overcome our worries by focusing on the present moment. When we concentrate on living purposefully each moment, we let go of our past and future. We waste enormous amounts of time and energy worrying about what we did or didn't do in the past or might do in the future. We act productively by evaluating our past and planning for our future; we act counterproductively when we worry about controlling or changing them.

By deciding beforehand how much time we will spend on a particular problem, we enhance the achievement process in three ways. We focus with greater intensity during this time allotment than for an unlimited amount of time. We eliminate wasting more time on a problem than we feel it is worth. We avoid additional problems by making a decision within a reasonable amount of time.

We fail only when we don't try. By confronting our problems, we receive their inherent benefits. We learn new ideas when we try to solve the problem. We strengthen our human spirit by taking on new challenges and giving our very best toward achieving them.

Personal integrity serves as our spirit's preventive medicine. By eating properly and working out regularly, we keep some illnesses from occurring. When we do what we think is the

Problem Solvers

right thing to do, we prevent a number of problems from creeping into our spirit, personal life, relationships, and career. As long as we maintain our personal integrity, we have a starting point for achieving our goals.

Perseverance separates the people who work for a better life from those people who wouldn't mind getting there. After our enthusiasm wanes, our attitude doesn't know anymore, and the facts have been figured in, we achieve our biggest goals by continuing to move toward them. With old-fashioned tenacity and sustained effort, we break through rigid comfort zones, turn wonderful dreams into realities, and experience new joys.

When we genuinely smile, our muscles relax, tension leaves our body, and we approach our problem from the perspective of fun rather than stress. We feel like a child playing with toys and enjoy the problem rather than hating it.

When we write our problem down, we see the exact issue we're dealing with and start to derive specific solutions. We may realize this problem has nothing to do with our actual purpose. We see the problem in a new way and create new solutions. We may find out the problem doesn't exist. By defining the problem, we see what we need to work on and stop wasting time, money, and energy on superficial issues.

Many times we start out excited about our goal, but we end up thinking only about the obstacles we face. We lose our enthusiasm and want to give up. We step toward success by staying focused on our purposeful process and ignoring the people and circumstances trying to stop us.

We solve problems by looking for a better way than our original gameplan for reaching our objective. When we reflect on our situation, trust our intuition, and stay flexible, we may decide to change our process for a better method.

We increase our productive energies by detaching our focus from the results of our efforts. We move forward by giving

Problem Solvers

our best within the process of achieving our goal and not worrying about the results. We instill meaning into our life by reaching for a goal. By emotionally detaching ourself from the results, we increase the amount of energy we have to give toward achieving it.

When we approach problems courageously, we realize our addictions, magnets, and balloons and work to relinquish their control over us. We endure the painful and humbling experience of admitting we made a mistake. We stand up for our beliefs in the midst of potentially losing our job or the support of our friends. We admit when we need the help of a higher power to see us through our problems.

Sometimes our best move is to pull back from one goal to avoid going broke or insane and move in a new direction. When we step back, we do so with a victory rather than a defeat. We learned new information for solving a variety of other problems by aspiring toward our original goal. Even though from an outside-in perspective we hate to admit we're pulling back, we enhance our ability to fulfill our purpose by shifting to a different goal.

We put our past "failures" to good use when we turn the objectives we didn't reach into inspiration for overcoming future obstacles. When we recall these past frustrations, we drive ourself further than we ever thought possible.

Sometimes our difficulties seem overwhelming. We solve the big puzzle one piece at a time by breaking our big problems down into smaller parts. We approach the easy victories first and build toward the more challenging ones.

We compile a list of possible solutions by writing the problem down and brainstorming for every idea that comes to us regardless of how crazy it seems. Ideas will flow through us onto the paper. We even create solutions for future problems. We sift through these ideas after we finish compiling them.

Role models provide us with a great deal of useful

Problem Solvers

information. When we find someone who has already experienced our current challenges, we save time and energy by studying their successful and unsuccessful strategies.

We find solutions by writing our problem down in detail, placing this paper by our bed, and going to sleep. Rather than thinking about the problem, we fill our mind with pleasant thoughts and fall into a deep sleep. Meanwhile, our unconscious mind works on this problem and formulates an answer. When it delivers this solution to our conscious mind, we immediately write it down.

At times, we feel helpless. We don't see any way out of our problem. We may even consider suicide. If we believe in our purpose, trust a higher power, and follow our intuition, we will overcome this problem. We demonstrate our faith in a divine higher power by turning our decisions over to it. We no longer have to take on life and all of its challenges by ourself. When we allow this higher power to join us, we feel cared for and loved. We realize it's okay to turn our problems over to this divine energy. We move forward with less stress and pressure.

What problems are you facing right now and how will you solve them?

Achievement State Of Mind

We prepare for success by creating the Achievement State of Mind.

We create an Achievement State of Mind in two ways. In the first method, we use general success principles that I call Universal Symptoms of Success. In the second method, we use the success principles we developed in our previously successful situations that I call Personal Symptoms of Success.

Universal Symptoms of Success

Just as a car will not run without sparkplugs, we will not achieve our goals without some internal fire. We develop this flame by finding a reason for choosing an activity. Whether we take out the garbage, write a report, or talk with our teenage children, we either find a reason for doing the activity and feel purposeful or do not find a reason and feel meaningless.

When we wash our car, cut the lawn, or clean up our house, we step further into the Achievement State of Mind by visualizing exactly what we want the finished product to look like. With this mental picture in front of us, we move steadily toward accomplishing it. By visualizing the end at the beginning, we keep our mind focused, gather our resources, and apply them toward accomplishing our objectives.

If we pour our energies into our activities and detach our thoughts from other distractions, we enhance our process. When children play a game, they invest all of their attention in their activities and have no concerns with any outside distractions. Children enter the proper mental environment for reaching their goals without even realizing it.

We strengthen our state of mind by involving every dimension of our human spirit in the activity. Every event has the potential to involve all four dimensions. Before we do something, we analyze why we want to do it, arrive at a purpose,

Achievement State Of Mind

and express this purpose through our personality.

Feedback helps us stay mentally alert. We evaluate our situation by continually gathering information during the activity. We invent ways for gathering information in every situation. We count the number of dishes we wash and dry in a given number of minutes, outline the ideas we learn from a certain author, or tune into the feelings we experience while loving another person. We evaluate this information by asking ourself, "Am I on the right path for reaching my definite purpose?" After the evaluation, we outline options for reaching our objective and choose one or two of them.

We step into the Achievement State of Mind faster by making the activity a steady routine. If long periods of time elapse between doing the activity, we spend a lot of energy relearning what needs to be done. When we create a routine for doing our activity, we jump right in, pick up where we left off, and avoid wasting time or energy.

The word "enthusiasm" comes from the Greeks and means "The God within". When we act with enthusiasm, we release the energy of a higher power within us and allow it to flow toward the realization of our objective.

When our current skills reasonably match those required for the activity, we feel more confident about reaching our goals. We steadily increase our skills by taking on ever increasing challenges. If we approach goals that require much more or much less than our current skills will handle, we enter the Failure State of Mind or Bored State of Mind. As our skills improve, we challenge them with more demanding objectives.

By applying these general principles, we experience the tremendous joy of investing our energy in activities that interest us. We create our self-contained world and feel purposeful, fulfilled, and in control. We gain a sense of adventure and stop worrying about what other people think. We move from

Achievement State Of Mind

constantly staring at a clock and hoping the activities would end to enjoying the process of reaching our goals.

Personal Symptoms of Success

We create the Achievement State of Mind by using our own principles of success. First, we identify situations from our past where we felt extremely successful and capable of high achievement and other situations where we experienced low levels of self-confidence and felt incapable of even mediocre achievement. Second, we analyze what we thought, felt, and did in each situation. Third, we replace our symptoms of failure with our symptoms of success.

If we had an out-of-body experience and could observe ourself from a distance in both our successful and unsuccessful situations, how would we describe what we saw? Did we appear confident, peaceful, worried, concerned, at ease, amused, bothered, or excited? By using as many descriptive words as possible, we capture the way we externalize our feelings. The way we project our emotions sends a message to our mind that we feel capable or incapable of achieving success.

We gain more personal clues by turning inward and recalling our actual feelings during each type of activity. We move to new heights by riding the crest of enhancing emotions or we paralyze ourself with restricting emotions.

What specific phrases did we say in each of these situations? What key words did we use over and over? How did we describe our efforts when we discussed this situation with another person? The language we use tells our mind that we either believe we will succeed or fail.

How did we physically act in both scenarios? How did we stand and sit? How did we use our arms and hands? Did we move slowly, carefully, nervously, quickly, with short steps, or long strides? Did we talk fast, slow, loud, or soft? Our physical actions record our state of mind. When we substitute our movements from our highly self-confident situations into our low self-confident situations, we impact our mental attitude. We send a message of confidence to our minds by doing something as simple as sitting up straight or slouching over.

What did we concentrate on while experiencing each scenario? Did we zero in on another person's eyes, certain sounds, particular colors, or a specific feeling?

What experiences did we recall when we were in each of the situations? Did we remember times when we felt excited, embarrassed, prepared, or successful? The memories we refer back to prepare our minds for success or failure. By recalling self-motivating memories in the moment leading up to our activity, we enhance our self-confidence.

What essence did we bring into our successful and unsuccessful experiences? We attached values, desired outcomes, and constructed rules that led to one state of mind or the other. After we identify our essence in each scenario, we choose the governing energies that helped us in the past.

Once we familiarize ourself with our personal symptoms, we replace our symptoms of failure with our symptoms of success. We use the perceptions, feelings, language, actions, points of focus, memories, and essence from our highly confident situations in the situations where we doubted ourself. As soon as we begin shifting our state of mind from one perspective to the other, we begin building the Achievement State of Mind one piece at a time where the Failure State of Mind once stood.

How will you apply the Universal Symptoms of Success and your Personal Symptoms of Success to your most meaningful goal?

Actitudes

Actitudes combine self-enhancing actions and attitudes.

We reinforce specific aspects of our spirit by combining enriching attitudes with their correlating actions.

When we encounter another person walking down the hallway, we look up, smile, and say,"Hello, how are you? Have a nice day." By doing this, we recognize our own dignity and the dignity of another person.

When we open a door to enter a building, we hold it for the next person even if they are fifteen feet behind us. By holding the door in a polite manner and not signaling them to hurry, we demonstrate the value we see in the other person.

When we clean up our desk, room, car, or home, we take charge of our day. We realize our capacity for reaching our other goals by completing these projects. When we read a book, cut the grass, or begin any activity, we strengthen our self-confidence by finishing it.

We take control of our attitude by working very passionately and with a great deal of enthusiasm. We turn what we used to dread into something fun and rewarding. We replace a negative with a positive by combining an action with the attitude of enjoying it.

When we turn inward and say positive comments about ourself for fifteen minutes, we invest in our self-improvement. We review our redeeming qualities and successful activities from the past week by making a list of the nice words someone said to us, good deeds we did for other people, books we read, actitudes we carried out, physical workouts we performed, and smiles we gave. In this way, we build our own inspirational story.

We create positive affirmations by making statements like,"I will enjoy this day and respect myself at the end of it" and "I will make my dreams come true".

Actitudes

When we approach every person we meet from the perspective of kindness and caring, we help them develop their human spirit. When we give a kind word, a gentle touch, and several moments of empathetic listening, we convey the message that all people are important.

When we stay away from our radios, newspapers, and magazines, we save time for complete silence. In this quiet space, we relax, slow down, and allow a sense of peacefulness to flow through us. We use this self-control to enhance our self-esteem and find added strength for living with integrity.

When we take care of our body, we feel better about ourself. We increase our self-confidence by doing aerobics, jogging, swimming, playing racquetball, lifting weights, or walking.

We emphasize the belief that we have inherent value by saying goodbye to an old friend: the television set! By turning off our television set at 6:00 PM and leaving it off for the rest of the evening, we realize that we, rather than the television, control our decisions.

When we take responsibility for a situation, we strengthen our self-confidence. Whether we're at home or at work, we mature by fulfilling our promises within a reasonable amount of time.

By saying, "Please, thank you, yes, ma'am, and no, sir" at the appropriate time, we acknowledge the dignity of another person. By acting in a polite way toward others, we see ourself as a caring individual.

We increase our self-confidence by living according to our own principles. If we believe that honesty should be used in every situation and find ourself in a very touchy situation, we strongly affect our current level of self-confidence by the way we respond. If we remain honest, we see ourself as a good and honest person. If we lie, we tarnish our self-image.

Actitudes

When we volunteer our services to another person or organization, we show how much we believe in our own abilities. We demonstrate the value we have to offer other human beings by giving our time, energy, and talents to them.

We develop strong self-confidence through continual practice. We hone our skills in singing, dancing, athletics, speaking, selling, writing, or dealing with other people through many hours of practice. As we practice a particular skill, we look for ways of improving our previous methods. By combining a desire to improve with the physical action of practicing, we strengthen our belief in this particular objective.

We re-energize our spirit by doing a variety of actions. We balance ourself when we exercise, walk quietly, read a book, write a letter, go the extra mile in our job, cuddle up with our significant other, playfully wrestle with children, and pray.

We show how much we value young people by genuinely investing our time and talent with them. By truly listening to a child or an adolescent, we give a tremendous gift to them and us. We help them see their inherent worth. We also see ourself as a loving person.

We reinforce our own dignity by rewarding our efforts. We may go on a special date, spend some time alone, read a book, or go to a party. When we combine effort with reward, we avoid burnout. We gain very little by going as fast as possible for a relatively short period of time only to end up quitting altogether. We maintain freshness in our work by pulling back and smelling the roses from time to time.

We take the first step toward creating the day we really desire by writing down exactly what we want to achieve. Our goals might include maintaining the attitude we want, finishing a project, improving a relationship, or clarifying certain ideas.

Some of us make this the "hurry up society". When we speed along, we rarely get enough sleep. We fear missing out

Actitudes

on something important. This lack of sleep keeps us from reaching our full potential. When we sleep for a sufficient amount of time, we improve the quality of what we do.

We make a special impact on other people by genuinely saying the words, "I love you." We expose our inner self and present our feelings in an extraordinarily vulnerable way.

We show how much we appreciate the precious gift of life by slowing down and enjoying it. When we quit sprinting to the next meeting, class, project, game, and sale, we take control of our life. We slow down by enjoying the things we used to rush through. We relax during our shower, smile through traffic, and chuckle when someone else frantically runs around.

We increase our self-confidence by reading about and listening to successful achievers. Achievers come in all shapes and sizes and from every conceivable background. When we see how they've made it, we start to believe we will achieve our dreams as well. If we read a book or listen to a tape about someone or by someone who has successfully reached his objectives, we gather ideas for achieving our goals.

We hurt our efforts by taking the "exception". Statements like "I'll just eat one piece of pizza", "One sick day won't damage my career", and "Just looking at another person won't hurt my marriage" focus our attention on possible exceptions to our plans. These exceptions keep us from getting what we want. We multiply our achievements by sticking to our plans and avoiding exceptions.

What actitudes will you use today to enhance your self-confidence?

Success Maintenance

We maintain success by reviewing our past and planning for our future.

We maintain a successful life by answering our own set of daily, weekly, and yearly "check-up questions".

We focus on meaningful objectives through our daily questions. Some examples include, "Did I take care of and improve my spirit, mind, body, and personality today?", "Did I show respect for myself and every person I met today?", and "Did I enhance my career today?" Based on our answers, we may alter our daily actions.

Alcoholics Anonymous experiences great success in helping its members stay sober by having weekly meetings. Individuals remain conscious of turning their lives over to a higher power and avoiding their first drink by talking with other members on a weekly basis. The same principle holds when two people meet every week to remain conscious of what they want to achieve, how they are doing in the pursuit of their goals, and what they will do to improve their performances in the future.

My best friend, Jeff Hutchison, and I get together every year for a "Dream Weekend". On Friday evening and Saturday morning, we discuss the times we felt successful during the past year in developing our personal lives, relationships, and careers. On Saturday afternoon and evening, we discuss the times we felt unsuccessful in reaching our objectives. On Sunday morning, we write down our goals for the upcoming year. On Sunday afternoon, we discuss these goals with each other. This experience helps us see the direction we are heading in, identify our objectives for the next year, and improve our methods for reaching these objectives.

How will you maintain your success?

Widening Our Comfort Zone

We widen our comfort zone by challenging our current way of thinking.

We stop cultivating our human spirit when we stop fueling our mind with new ideas and different ways of reinforcing old ideas. We expand our comfort zone by consistently studying new concepts.

We enhance our mind through reading because we take in the information at our own pace and clarify our opinions about the author's thoughts. While the author spent years selecting his or her unique ideas, we learn these concepts in just a few days or weeks of reading. We step into a "conversation" with the author and develop our own principles of success.

My "Library of Success" contains the books I've completely read on the topic of personal and organizational development. While reading these books, I experienced an adventure of the mind and spirit far exceeding anything I expected. I view these authors as my catalysts for living the life I consciously want to live.

Library of Success

Alcoholics Anonymous Alcoholics Anonymous
Allen, James As a Man Thinketh
Angelou, Maya Wouldn't Take Nothing for My Journey Now
Anthony, Robert
     The Ultimate Secrets of Total Self-Confidence
Bach, Richard Jonathan Livingston Seagull
     The Bridge Across Forever
     One
     Illusions
     There's No Such Place as Far Away
     Running from Safety
Beattie, Melody Codependent No More
     The Lessons of Love
Bennis, Warren Leaders (with **Nanus, Bert**)
     On Becoming a Leader

Widening Our Comfort Zone

Bhagavad-Gita, The (translated by **Barbara Stoler Miller**)
Blanchard, Ken
        The One Minute Manager (**with Johnson, Spencer**)
        Everyone's a Coach (**with Shula, Don**)
Bloomfield, Harold and Vettese, Sirah   Lifemates
Branden, Nathaniel The Six Pillars of Self Esteem
Brown, Les Live Your Dreams
Bynham, William and Cox, Jeff
        Zapp: The Lightning of Empowerment
Cameron, Julia and Bryan, Mark The Artist's Way
Campbell, Joseph (selected by Diane Osbon)
        Reflections on the Art of Living
Carnegie, Dale How to Win Friends and Influence People
Carr, Pat In Her Image
Carson, Ben Think Big
Chopra, Deepak Creating Affluence
        The Seven Spirtual Laws of Success
        Perfect Health
        Return of the Rishi
Clark, Ronald Einstein: The Life and Times
Clason, George The Richest Man in Babylon
Collier, Robert Riches Within Your Reach
Conn, Charles Paul The Winner's Circle
Cooper, Ken The Aerobics Program for Total Well-Being
Covey, Stephen   Principle-Centered Leadership
        The Seven Habits of Highly Effective People
        First Things First (**with Merrill, Roger and Rebecca**)
Csikszentmihalyi, Mihaly
        Flow: Psychology of Optimal Experience
Dass, Ram Journey of Awakening
Deming, W. Edwards Out of the Crisis
DePree, Max Leadership as an Art
DeVos, Rich Believe (**with Charles Paul Conn**)
        Compassionate Capitalism
Dooley, Thomas and Agnes Promises to Keep
Dyer, Wayne Your Erroneous Zones
        Real Magic
        You'll See It When You Believe It
        The Sky's the Limit
        Gifts from Eykis
Edelman, Marian Wright The Measure of Our Success

Widening Our Comfort Zone

Elkind, David The Hurried Child
Gandhi, Mohandas Gandhi: An Autobiography
Gawain, Shakti Creative Visualization
   Living in the Light
   Return to the Garden
   The Path of Transformation
Gibran, Kahlil The Prophet
Givens, Charles Superself
Goddard, Neville Awakened Imagination
   The Power of Awareness
Goldratt, Eliyahu The Goal (**with Cox, Jeff**)
   It's Not Luck
   Theory of Constraints
Hansen, Mark Victor and Canfield, Jack Dare to Win
   Chicken Soup for the Soul
Hedges, Burke Who Stole the American Dream
Hendrix, Harville Getting the Love You Want
   Keeping the Love You Find
Hoff, Benjamin The Tao of Pooh
   The Te of Piglet
Hill, Napolean Grow Rich with Peace of Mind
   Law of Success
   The Master Key to Riches
   Think and Grow Rich
   You Can Work Your Own Miracles
Hill, Napolean and Stone, W. Clement
   Success Through a Positive Mental Attitude
Holmes, Ernest This Thing Called You
   This Thing Called Life
Iacocca, Lee Iacocca: An Autobiography
   Straight Talk
Johnson, John Succeeding Against the Odds
Jones, Laurie Beth Jesus: CEO
Jordan, Michael I Can't Accept Not Trying
Josephson, Matthew Edison: A Biography
Keller, Helen The Story of My Life
King, Martin Luther (**selected by Coretta Scott King**)
   The Words of Martin Luther King
Kohe, J. Martin Your Greatest Power
Kornhaber, Arthur Spirit
Lee, John The Flying Boy

Widening Our Comfort Zone

Maltz, Maxwell Pscychocybernetics
Mandino, Og A Better Way to Live
        The Gift of Acabar
        The Choice
        Mission: Success
        The Greatest Salesman in the World
        The Greatest Salesman in the World: Part II
        The Greatest Miracle in the World
        University of Success
        The Twelfth Angel
        The Spellbinder's Gift
        The Christ Commission
Maxwell, John Developing the Leaders Around You
May, Rollo Man's Search for Himself
McClung, Floyd Finding Friendship with God
McCormack, John and Legge, David
        Self-Made in America
Merton, Thomas No Man is an Island
Millman, Dan Way of the Peaceful Warrior
        Sacred Journey of the Peaceful Warrior
Morgan, Marlo Mutant Message Down Under
Nightingale, Earl The Essence of Success
Peale, Norman Vincent The Power of Positive Thinking
Peck, Scott The Road Less Traveled
        Further Along the Road Less Traveled
        A World Waiting to be Born
Petersen, Donald Teamwork
Pirsig, Robert Zen and the Art of Motorcycle Maintenance
Powell, John Happiness is an Inside Job
Rademacher, Mary Anne Live with Intention
Ray, Veronica A Design for Growth
Redfield, James The Celestine Prophecy
Riley, Pat The Winner Within
Ringer, Robert Million Dollar Habits
Ritt, Michael and Landers, Kirk
        A Lifetime of Riches: The Biography of Napolean Hill
Robbins, Anthony Unlimited Power
        Awaken the Giant Within
St. James, Elaine Inner Simplicity
        Simplify Your Life

Widening Our Comfort Zone

Schuller, Robert
     Success is Never Ending, Failure is Never Final
     Reach out for New Life
Schutz, Susan Polis Don't Ever Stop Dreaming Your Dreams
Schwartz, David The Magic of Thinking Big
Schweitzer, Albert (edited by Thomas Kiernan)
     A Treasury of Albert Schweitzer
Seuss, Dr. Oh, The Places You'll Go
Shinn, Florence The Game of Life (And How to Play It)
Siegel, Bernie Love, Medicine, and Miracles
Singletary, Mike Singletary on Singletary
Smith, Hyrum The Ten Natural Laws of Successful Time and
     Life Management
Stone, W. Clement The Success System That Never Fails
Thomas, Bob Walt Disney: An American Original
Thoreau, Henry David Walden
Tzu, Lao Tao Te Ching **(translated by Victor Mair)**
Waller, Robert James Old Songs in a New Cafe
     Border Music
Walton, Mary The Deming Management Method
Walton, Sam Made in America
Weinhaus, Evonne and Friedman, Karen
     Stop Struggling with Your Child
     Stop Struggling with Your Teen
Williams, A. L. All You Can Do is All You Can Do, But All You
     Can Do is Enough
Williams, Pat Go for the Magic
Williamson, Marianne A Return to Love
     A Woman's Worth
Wills, Garry Certain Trumpets: The Nature of Leadership
Wooden, John They Call Me Coach
Wooten, Morgan From Orphans To Champions
Yager, Dexter and Ball, Ron
     Ordinary Men, Extraordinary Heroes
Ziglar, Zig See You at the Top

Widening Our Comfort Zone

We widen our comfort zone by developing all of our senses. If we study automobiles, we listen for certain noises, smell the engine, look at the transmission fluid, and run our hands over the interior. While on vacation, we smell the new environment, look at the scenery, taste the specialty foods, and listen to the unique sounds.

Even if we excel in one external role or internal dimension, we mature by striving to develop all of them. If we focus on one dimension or role and ignore the rest, we limit ourself. People committed to expanding their comfort zones search for ways to develop each of their roles and dimensions.

When we learn one new idea from every person we meet, we rapidly develop as an individual. We derive many ideas by simply listening to other people. Their memories enrich us by causing us to think about our situations. We learn from the mistakes and successes of other people without having to personally experience all of their careers and relationships.

We turn our life into a daily classroom situation by searching for new ideas and applying them toward our goals. Successful students take very good notes. We do the same thing by writing down new ideas in our "Life's Educational Notebook". We learn these ideas from other people, books, television programs, and our own experiences. Ideas come to us in the form of quotes, stories, or analogies. We capture the new ideas on paper in a few short sentences. Our "homework" consists of finding real-life applications for these new principles. Our "test" occurs when we use these principles in real-life situations and see how well they work.

As a math teacher, my students repeatedly ask me,"Why do we have to learn this?" The quadratic formula and trigonometric functions don't seem very important to them in their day-to-day lives. Every time they ask, I lower my voice, look straight at them, and say,"You will never, ever use this

Widening Our Comfort Zone

information again the rest of your lives." This statement usually quiets them down for awhile. After this comment, I say,"By learning how to learn, you gain a tremendously valuable tool for taking on other problems." In school, we have the opportunity to develop our communication skills, logical and intuitive thought processes, and problem-solving capacities.

We learn in non-graded courses as well. We expand our comfort zone by taking piano and dance lessons, public speaking courses, financial management seminars, cooking classes, and self-help workshops.

We extract many useful ideas from audiotapes and videotapes. By using these tools, we turn every waking moment into an opportunity for growth. We learn ideas by listening to audiotapes while we cut the grass, drive our car, wash the dishes, or do the laundry. Instead of watching a television program, we learn by renting a video by an expert in our field of interest.

When we ask questions, we discover valuable information. "How did this person achieve so much success? Why did that person fail? Why was this the right answer and that the wrong one? How does this system work? What would be a better way of doing this? How will I increase my effectiveness and efficiency?" These questions expand our mind.

When we try, we may "fail" from an outside-in perspective. However, if we learn at least one important lesson from the experience, we move closer to achieving our objective. If we try again, we may fail again, but that's alright. With each attempt, we grow in at least one way. We widen our comfort zone by saying to ourself,"Make a mistake, learn. Make a mistake, learn. Make a ..."

What will you do to widen your comfort zone?

Choosing Our Cornerstones

Our human spirit, personal life, relationships, and career form our individual building. We create a signifcant life by carefully deciding how we will live both internally and externally. These decisions represent the cornerstones that we construct our building on. When we choose them, we decide what our life stands for. The questions in the following three chapters help us derive them. After reflecting on these questions and listening to our intuition, we write down three guiding statements. We don't need to judge our actions and efforts by any standards other than our own cornerstones. However, we don't write these statements in concrete. We can revise them. Integrity involves living according to our present understanding of life. As our awareness expands, we may decide to alter our cornerstones in order to maintain our personal integrity.

Crusades

Our crusades represent what we stand for regarding our spirit, mind, personality, and body.

People on a crusade expend extraordinary levels of commitment and creativity in trying to reach their objectives. They tap into resources of energy they would otherwise never touch. They reach further and give more of themselves than they ever thought possible. They develop an inner strength that enables them to achieve beyond their wildest dreams. Mohandas Gandhi crusaded for the people of India. Martin Luther King, Jr. used nonviolent protests to crusade against racism. Candy Leitner started Mothers Against Drunk Driving and altered our society's viewpoint on drinking and driving. Crusaders direct their energy toward what they consider a worthy cause. When we crusade to develop our human spirit, we enhance our ability to reach our goals. We don't have to wait for an external cause to enhance our internal dimensions.

How will you strengthen your spirit? What governing energies will guide your decisions? What ideas will you pursue? How will you enhance your mind on a daily basis? How will your personality express your thoughts? Will you be more aggressive, outspoken, tender, honest, or in tune with your true feelings? Will you be less solution-oriented and more supportive of other people's ideas or just the opposite? In your intimate relationships, will you be less sexual and more sensual, more giving and less taking, more other-person centered and less self-centered, or the opposite of these? What will you stand for in terms of enhancing your body? What specific physical objectives will you have?

Daily Intentions

Our daily intentions represent what we stand for in our personal life, relationships, and career.

We perform certain roles in the theater of life. We either deliberately choose how we act or our subconscious makes these choices for us. Our daily intentions state how we consciously choose to perform our external roles. When we answer the following questions, we decide how we will act before the day starts and avoid blindly following other people.

What will you concentrate on in your personal life? How will you express your thoughts to your spouse or significant other? How about with your parents, children, and siblings? How will you act toward and communicate with your friends? How will you interact with your managers, peers, and subordinates? What will your career stand for? What will you contribute within your career? What other roles do you act out everyday? How do you identify your role within your city, country, or society? Do you belong to a special interest group? What will your purpose be within each of these roles? How will you fulfill these objectives?

Life's Main Purpose

We identify our life's main purpose by reflecting on our essence and trusting our intuition.

"If I build it, he will come. Go the distance. Ease his pain." Ray Kinsella heard these words from the voice in the film "Field Of Dreams". By listening to and acting on these words, Ray found his life's main purpose. He built a baseball field in the middle of a corn patch. He didn't understand this purpose right away, but in the end he created a place where adults relived their childhood. They experienced the sense of wonder of innocent, wide-eyed children. Even though other people laughed at him, Ray followed through on his intuition and achieved internal and external success.

Even if we do not clearly see our life's main purpose, we begin to identify it by writing down what we feel inside of us right now. We may need several years to mold and perfect our statement. We may start out with several paragraphs and eventually sharpen it to a single sentence. I went through this process. I wanted an umbrella statement that covered all of my most important values and desires. My original statement was four paragraphs long. It included years, ages, dollar figures, names of people, and all sorts of other external information. After three years, I narrowed my life's main purpose to one sentence:

My main purpose is to actually live the life I consciously want to live and help other people do the same thing.

What message is your inner voice delivering to you right now? What is your life's main purpose?

Moving Into The Light

At the beginning of this book, I described the difference between inside-out and outside-in thinking as the difference between going after our objectives in a room filled with light as opposed to a completely darkened room. This section contains ideas on setting specific monthly, yearly, five year, and ten year goals. When we deliberately select our goals, we move further into the light of conscious living.

Building Our Window Of Significance

We clarify our most meaningful short-term goals through our window of significance.

Imagine we are standing in the middle of a house with a large window on each of its four sides. Through the first window, we see large trees and flowers of all types. Through the second window, we see people shooting guns and screaming at one another. Through the third window, we see well-trimmed lawns and moderately priced automobiles. Through the fourth window, we see a huge mansion with a Mercedes-Benz parked in front of it. We vary our objectives according to the window we look through. We may want to spend time alone, call the police, talk with our neighbors, or buy a Cadillac.

From an internal perspective, we see our goals through our "window of significance". We build this window by drawing a rectangle in the middle of a piece of paper. We write one of our external roles at the top of the page and our specific crusades, daily intentions, and life's main purpose for this particular external role at the bottom of the page. We write our specific short-term goals for this external role in our window of significance. If we need more room, we make our window of significance on another piece of paper. I suggest we start with two or three specific goals for each of the first few months.

At the end of the month, we use this tool to evaluate how we have done. Did our actions and efforts fit in with our cornerstones? Did we stay focused on our goals or did we do what other people told us to do? Did we reach our goals? After we evaluate the previous month's efforts, we look through this special window to set our goals for the next month. I've included an example for you to get some ideas from and a page to copy.

What goals will you place in your window of significance?

My External Role
(personal life, relationships, or career)

relationship with co-workers

> • listen empathetically for twenty minutes daily
>
> • write a note 3 times a week telling other people how special they are
>
> • get the proper amount of sleep each night so I have energy to give to other people

My Window of Significance

My Crusades: spirit : clarify my essence during conversations
mind : learn from every person I meet
personality : focus on the other person's
body : express openness to feelings
new ideas and interest in other person

My Daily Intentions:
"tune in" to other people and be there for them. Place greater value on relationships than accomplishments.

My Life's Main Purpose:
Live the life I consciously want to live and help other people do the same thing

99

My External Role
(personal life, relationships, or career)

My Window of Significance

My Crusades:

My Daily Intentions:

My Life's Main Purpose:

Perfect Year

We base our year-long goals on our perfect year.

What would have to happen today for us to consider it a perfect day? Would we wake up without an alarm clock, spend time with our family and friends, or do some reading, writing, and walking?

In order to create a perfect week, do we want to meet an old friend we haven't seen for years, give a powerful talk on a meaningful topic, or sneak away for a romantic vacation?

What do we require for a perfect year? Do we want to accomplish one of our life-long dreams, reconcile with a friend over an incident that happened years ago, or improve our relationships by listening better. When we write down exactly what our perfect year will be like in terms of our human spirit, personal life, relationships, career, and life's main purpose, we step toward creating the reality we want. After we write these perfect year statements, we set specific goals that fit into these statements. If our perfect year includes getting together with an old friend and talking about the problems in our relationship, we write as one of our goals to contact this person and set up a time to meet. An example might look like this:

Perfect Year

Role: Friend

Perfect Year Statement: I am much closer to my old friend. We talk about meaningful issues and resolve old problems. We communicate openly with each other.

Goals: Call my friend. Ask to spend time with him at a special location. Set up a specific time and location. When we get together, we will talk through our problems and rekindle our friendship.

What does your perfect year look like?

Personal National Championship

When we go after our personal national championship, we focus our energies on one major, year-long objective.

In the spring of 1991, I watched the semifinal game of the NCAA Division I Men's Basketball Tournament between the University of Nevada-Las Vegas and Duke University. Even though Duke lost to UNLV by thirty points in the 1990 championship game, I cheered for Duke to win this game. The lead went back and forth throughout the game, but in the end Duke won this game as well as the championship game two nights later. I started running around my apartment and yelling as loud as I could. UNLV had not lost a game the entire season, and yet somehow Duke had beaten them. I thought to myself,"I would love to be on this team. They prepared for an entire year to achieve this objective. They focused all of their efforts on winning these two games. It all came down to one weekend where they could win or lose the national championship."

The more I thought about being on Duke's team, the more depressed I became. I had resigned as a college head coach the year before. As a head coach, I dreamed of winning a national championship. When I left college coaching, I thought I had to leave this dream behind me. After a few minutes of feeling sorry for myself, I thought,"Wait a second. Why couldn't all people choose one major, year-long goal in any area of their lives and make it their personal national championship? On the final day of the goal, they would either win or lose their own national championship. In this way, every person would experience the same challenges, setbacks, and thrills that the Duke University team experienced."

In my first national championship, I lost twenty-five pounds. In my second quest for a personal national championship, I unsuccessfully tried to teach my course on

Personal National Championship

success principles to three hundred people. In the third year, I tried to establish balance throughout my entire life. This year, my personal national championship is to write and publish this book. Sometimes I win my personal national championship and sometimes I lose. No matter what happens the previous year, I always set my major, year-long goal and fuel myself with excitement and motivation by going after it.

Rather than waiting for someone else to construct a national tournament for us, we build our own championship contest. Rather than competing against someone else, we operate on our personal initiative. What will we choose as this year's personal national championship? After we select our most important year-long goal, we apply all of the success principles in this book toward achieving it. We write detailed answers to the Quality Questions, list the personal powers we will use to attain this goal, and write down our specific Core Assets that will help us win. We identify any balloons we need to release and the aspects of our core we need to complete in order to achieve our personal national championship. We reflect on what needs to be done and trust our intuition. We identify the actitudes that will help us during the next year. We use the Universal Symptoms of Success and our own Personal Symptoms of Success to help us build the Achievement State of Mind. We create a future reality for this goal. We decide which problem solvers to use in dealing with our obstacles. We write specific success maintenance questions to help us win and keep on winning.

By going after our personal national championship, not only will we experience the excitement that the Duke University team experienced, but we will develop our success principles as well.

What is your personal national championship going to be for this year?

Five Year Blueprint

Our five year blueprint provides us with a structure for reaching our long-term goals.

Imagine someone asked us five years ago to construct a city from the ground up. We jumped into this project with extraordinary levels of energy and dedication. At the end of five years, we created the city we always wanted. We built magnificent centers for industry, technology, entertainment, and the fine arts. Modern schools, spectacular athletic facilities, and brand new homes add beauty to the surroundings. Except, what if we forgot about the transportation system? What if we didn't plan for the streets and highways? Instead of achieving great success, we created a huge mess. Rather than feeling pleased with our accomplishments, we experience a sense of deep despair.

We create this frustrating scenario in real-life situations by pouring huge amounts of time, energy, and effort into achieving our dreams before we have a blueprint for reaching them. We enhance our chances for success by designing our own five year blueprint. We begin designing our blueprint by examining our essence. Based on our values, beliefs, principles, desires, and cornerstones, we derive our "five year goals" for each dimension of our human spirit and every one of our external roles. We create our actual blueprint by answering the quality questions for each of these goals. With a deliberately developed and flexible plan, we confidently build the life we want.

When will you start creating your five year blueprint?

A Decade Of Achievement

We build our decade of achievement by seeing our future achievements as clearly as our past accomplishments.

We review our Decade of Accomplishment by thinking about the past year in terms of our roles and the dimensions of our human spirit. What did we accomplish in each of these areas? As we mentally relive one accomplishment, we remember another. After this past year soaks into our mind, we write down all of our accomplishments. When we finish writing about the past year, we reach back to two years ago and do the same thing. By continuing backward for each of the last ten years and concentrating on our accomplishments, we develop a peak performance state of mind. The past ten years represent our Decade of Accomplishment. By looking at old notes, newspaper articles, photo albums, videotapes, and photographs, we remember our large and small achievements. We rekindle the exhilirating feeling of reaching our goals.

After we review the Decade of Accomplishment, we prelive the next ten years, our Decade of Achievement. We mentally step forward to one year from today. What "did" we achieve in our roles and within our human spirit during the past year? We mentally experience these future realities and enjoy these "memories". We visualize ourself living our dreams with enthusiasm and evolving to our fullest potential. When we do this for each of the next ten years, we choose the direction we want for our life. With these visualizations supporting us, we walk boldly into the light of conscious living and move forward from the inside-out.

What do your Decades of Accomplishment and Achievement look like?

EPILOGUE

A Society Dying To Grow

Some people say our society dies a little bit more each day. I agree with them more often than not. When fifty percent of all marriages end in divorce, some high school graduates can't read, many children are rushed into adult roles long before they are ready for them, and teenage pregnancies, suicides, and gang violence continually increase, I believe our society is eroding away at a rapid pace. However, just as an acorn must stop being an acorn for an oak tree to grow, and a caterpillar must stop being a caterpillar in order for a butterfly to take off, I believe we must let go of the old patterns of our society in order for a higher way of living to evolve. We have torn down some old, subconscious ways of prejudging and labeling people, and we must continue to do more of this. I believe we move our society to a higher way of living by stepping forward as inside-out leaders.

Leading From The Inside-Out

Robert Frost said he was walking one day in the woods and came to a fork in the road. He had to choose one path over the other. He stepped back, looked down both pathways, and noticed more people had walked down one of them because it was more worn out than the other path. He chose the road less traveled, and it made all the difference in his life. We face a fork in the road of our life every single day. The two paths are marked "outside-in" and "inside-out".

People who choose the road marked "outside-in" constantly worry about what other people think. They worry that other people won't accept them for who they really are. They change what they stand for, believe in, and desire whenever they face criticism or conflicting opinions. They alter what they think, do, and say based on how other people evaluate them.

People who choose the road less traveled live their lives from the inside-out. They consciously decide what they believe in, value, and desire. After they listen to other people's ideas and gather information, they deliberately form their own principles and base their decisions on these self-determined standards. They believe character is more important than reputation because character is who they really are while reputation is merely what other people think of them. They realize their unique inner gifts and send them outward. A special subgroup of inside-out thinkers are inside-out leaders. These people lead our society to a higher level.

What makes an inside-out leader? Inside-out leaders have five basic characteristics: First, they care about their own well-being and the well-being of other people. They concentrate on enhancing their own lives and the lives of other people. Second, they stand for something. They have a definite purpose in everything they do, and they stick to it regardless of what other people say. Third, they communicate what they stand for to other people. They let other people know what their purpose is, what they believe in, and what they value. Fourth, they live with integrity. They do what they think is the right thing to do at that given moment even if other people criticize, ridicule, or abandon them. Fifth, they project themselves consistently in every walk of life. They speak the same message to all of the diverse people they encounter on a daily basis.

What is the external look of an inside-out leader? Are they a certain size, color, race, sex, or religious member? We find the answer by examining some of the most famous inside-out leaders over the past one hundred and fifty years.

This inside-out leader lost her sight, hearing, and ability to speak at the age of three years old. Many people thought she would grow up to be an uneducated, feisty animal. Instead, she went on to study Latin, economics, and Elizabethan literature at Radcliffe University. She complained about college in the same way many non-handicapped people do. She said she was so busy taking notes and studying for tests that she had little time to really think. Helen Keller became a great inside-out leader because she stood for something. She believed physically handicapped people had just as much to offer society as anyone else. She cared about herself and other people. She communicated what she stood for through her books and lectures. She said,"The most beautiful things in life cannot be seen or touched, but are felt in the heart." She lived with integrity and projected herself consistently in everything she did.

Another inside-out leader from this time period seemed destined for failure. He was a very tall, slender man. He failed in business twice, lost in eight different political elections over a period of twenty-six years, and suffered a nervous breakdown after his girlfriend died. Yet, many people consider Abraham Lincoln to be our greatest president. Why? Because he stood for something. He believed that all people were created equal regardless of the color of their skin. He cared about all people

Leading From The Inside-Out

because everyone is a human being. He believed that no person had the right to own another person. He communicated his beliefs and maintained his stance even as the country surged into a civil war. Abraham Lincoln lived with integrity and projected his beliefs consistently even though it cost him his life.

Perhaps Abraham Lincoln inspired this great inside-out leader. He was a relatively short and very slender man. When he died, they put all of his material belongings on a table. He had a rice bowl, the white cloth he wore, and a pair of sandals. He had no title or financial control over other people. When he was in high school, he said the hardest thing he had to do was geometry. The first time he spoke to an audience, he stood up, looked at the people, and sat right back down. He was too nervous to speak. In spite of this, Mohandas Gandhi became one of the two or three greatest inside-out leaders the world has ever known. Mohandas Gandhi stood for something. He believed the people of India should be allowed to rule themselves. He stuck by his beliefs even while he spent many years in prison. He cared so deeply about himself and other people that he willingly gave himself up to be arrested. He communicated this message of freedom to the people of his nation and led them on a walk across the country to nonviolently protest against the British rulers. He lived with great personal integrity and refused to put certain substances into his body even though he almost starved to death. He projected his message consistently even though it cost him his life.

This inside-out leader was directly affected by Gandhi. He was an African-American who went to Montgomery, Alabama to be a preacher. He grew increasingly associated with the civil rights movement. He studied Gandhi's concept of nonviolent resistance and led other African-Americans to stand up to the white rulers of this country. Martin Luther King, Jr. stood for something. He dreamed that someday all children would join

Leading From The Inside-Out

hands and walk together. He believed people would eventually be judged by the content of their character rather than the color of their skin. He communicated his dream to anyone who would listen. He consistently did what he thought was the right thing to do. In the end, he increased our nation's consciousness and helped us move toward a higher way of living. Even though he died in the process, Martin Luther King, Jr. served this nation as a great inside-out leader.

In the late 1960's, this inside-out leader was considered to be the best center fielder in baseball. When he was traded from the St. Louis Cardinals to the Philadelphia Phillies, he refused to go. At that time, baseball owners literally owned the players for their entire careers. There was no such thing as free agency. Curt Flood said,"I am a person and a child of God. I am not a piece of meat to be bought and sold. I should be able to choose my employer just like every other businessman in this country." He took his case to the Supreme Court and lost. He was ostracized by the owners and never played, coached, or managed for any professional baseball organization again. He never received a dime for his efforts. Three years later the Supreme Court overturned its ruling and declared baseball players free agents. Curt Flood stood for something, cared about his rights and the rights of his fellow employees, communicated what he stood for, did what he thought was the right thing to do, and projected himself consistently to every person he met. As a result, one man changed baseball forever.

This inside-out leader never traveled more than two hundred miles from the place where he was born. He never visited a big city. He never held an office or owned a house. He worked in a carpenter shop until he was thirty years old. After this, he became an itinerant preacher. He never wrote a book and never went to college. However, he affected the lives of more people than all of the kings and presidents who have ever

Leading From The Inside-Out

lived. Jesus Christ influenced the world because he stood for something. He believed there was a much more meaningful life than accumulating material possessions and the praise of other people. He believed that internal development was more important than external acceptance. He taught people to take the bushel off their heads and let their unique light shine forth. He believed a higher power existed inside every one of us. He cared about his own internal life and the internal lives of every other person. He lived with integrity and communicated what he believed in to anyone who would listen. Jesus Christ was an inside-out leader who helped people realize that every individual is unique, special, and meaningful.

The moral of these stories is inside-out leaders come in all shapes, sizes, and colors, and from every race, religious background, profession, and walk of life. We evolve into inside-out leaders because of who we are on the inside, not on the outside.

Inside-out leaders are conscious warriors and creative artists. As conscious warriors, they make decisions with courage and compassion. They act with enthusiasm, decisiveness, faith, and commitment to a cause beyond their own personal gain. They draw on powers within themselves and direct them toward consciously selected purposes. They stand strong in the face of adversity and despair. As creative artists, inside-out leaders use their own success principles to strengthen and direct their human spirit in the same way artists carefully choose the various colors they paint onto a canvas. Life represents the canvas for inside-out leaders. They carefully, consciously, and creatively paint whatever picture they want in terms of developing their internal dimensions, external roles, and life's main purpose. Inside-out leaders do not use their success principles as a series of cookbook formulas. They carefully choose their colors in the order they need them.

Leading From The Inside-Out

What price do we have to pay if we decide to become inside-out leaders? The cost of inside-out leadership is a very high one. When we choose this role, we often experience the embarrassment of going after a definite objective and failing to attain it. We face the possibility of being abandoned by our family and friends for going after a purpose they disagree with. We sometimes lose income, employment, material possessions, and our reputations because of what we stand up for. Certain people will treat us as an outcast because of our choices. Just as Abraham Lincoln, Mohandas Gandhi, Martin Luther King, Jr., and Jesus Christ found out, we may even lose our life.

Why is becoming an inside-out leader worth it? The extraordinary effort it takes to become an inside-out leader is worth it because we know our life stands for something. We walk away from situations feeling we gave our very best to make a difference. If we choose to become inside-out leaders, we experience the exhilaration of pouring our efforts into what we consider a worthwhile cause and trying to turn this cause into a reality. We wake up each day and feel the excitement of going on a great adventure. We live valiantly as conscious warriors by fighting for what we believe in. We feel the excitement of trying to creatively come up with new, conscious solutions to old, subconscious challenges. We realize that temporary failure and ridicule do not overcome the incredible thrill of consciously identifying and fulfilling our unique purpose.

How do we get started on the path to becoming an inside-out leader? We take the first step by choosing our cornerstones and creating a foundation for our future decisions. On this foundation, we construct a meaningful life. The evolution of our society will happen when individuals take conscious control of their own life. We cannot wait for an external force to improve our society. We improve it by individually becoming inside-out leaders.

Leading From The Inside-Out

What do I stand for? I have tried to base my life on the cornerstones of personal integrity, doing what I thought was the right thing to do at that moment, and personal initiative, choosing my own direction rather than letting other people make this decision for me. When I failed to live according to these cornerstones and did not do what I thought was the right thing to do or let other people make my decisions for me, I felt the building of my life begin to crumble a little bit. When I really failed to live according to these cornerstones and blatantly did things that I knew were wrong or blindly followed other people's advice just so they would compliment me, I felt as though an earthquake had shattered my personal foundation. During these times, I knew I could not do anything meaningful with my life. When I have lived with integrity and made my own decisions, I felt my self-confidence and self-discipline grow stronger. During these times, I felt I could make a meaningful contribution toward helping other people live the life they consciously want to live.

Do we make our life easier by living consciously? I believe we make life more challenging when we realize we can take control of our own internal and external destiny and accept responsibility for our decisions. When we reach for our biggest dreams, we expend huge amounts of energy and commitment. We experience genuine exhaustion at the end of a day. If we prefer an "easy" life of just following orders and doing what we think others want us to do, we probably don't want to live consciously. If we want to enjoy the incredible feeling of a meaningful existence, we try to live the life we consciously want to live. Joseph Campbell said, "The privilege of a lifetime is being who we are." I believe we fulfill this privilege by consciously living with purpose from the inside-out.

If you are interested in ordering more copies of this book, call or write:

POS Publishing
P.O. Box 21814
St. Louis, MO 63109-0814
Phone (314)-453-8453